THE STAGE MANAGER'S HANDBOOK

The
STAGE

DBS PUBLICATIONS, INC.
Drama Book Specialists
New York, New York

MANAGER'S

HANDBOOK

By BERT GRUVER

THE STAGE MANAGER'S HANDBOOK

Copyright 1952, 1953 by ELBERT A. GRUVER, JR.

FIFTH PRINTING

Published by arrangement with

HARPER BROTHERS AND ELBERT A. GRUVER, JR.

Library of Congress catalog card number: 53-5370

Printed in the United States of America

CONTENTS

FOREWORD

A textbook on stage managing would be a monumental work, running to several volumes, because the stage manager's duties touch all production departments. Actually there is no need for such a book, since the bulk of it would be a duplication of material found in standard books on the theater. If the newcomer to Broadway is familiar with these standard books, or with such basic technique as he might acquire in a college drama department, a good summer or little theater, or a professional school, he will not require a textbook on stage managing. However, he may need a guidebook to help him utilize his basic knowledge in the stage manager's special field. This handbook has been written to supply that guide, and it should help the reader augment or consolidate his knowledge in terms of the Broadway production. A subtitle might be "A Method of Procedure for the Stage Manager of the Broadway or Touring Legitimate Play."

The stage manager's procedure, what his duties are, will be listed in detail. How he accomplishes those duties will be explained or illustrated only when standard books on the theater have ignored or neglected them. The *how's* are illustrative and must not be construed as being definitive. There is no limit to how a stage manager accomplishes his work except the limitations of the production itself and the extent of the stage manager's ingenuity.

INTRODUCTION

There are specialists in all branches of the theater, including stage managing. The actor is a specialist; so is the designer, the director, the stage hand, the playwright, and all other members of the production personnel. Practically all of these specialists have early training of some sort, serve an apprenticeship, before they achieve specialist standing. Many serve part of their apprenticeship as stage managers or more usually as assistant stage managers. It is uncommon to find a playwright whose early training has been designing, or a designer whose training has been writing. On the other hand, it is very common to find that both designer and playwright have served as an assistant stage manager. This is particularly true of the specialist who is an actor. An Actors' Equity rule permits the actor to occupy the dual role of understudy and/or actor and assistant stage manager. Consequently most producers require that one or more of their understudies be capable of serving as assistant stage managers, or, depending on one's point of view, that the assistant stage manager can understudy. And so one finds among assistant stage managers a transient population—a young and relatively inexperienced group, which will serve its apprenticeship and then pass on to specialties.

An individual assistant stage manager may consider his job a part of apprenticeship, a step toward a specialty other than stage managing, but that does not lessen the importance of the job. The normal assistant will want to do his work as well as he can. Certainly the producer will expect him to. The producer will understand his inexperience but will not forgive indifference. This handbook will help the ambitious apprentice understand the stage manager's problems and his methods of solving them.

A casual and generally accepted definition of the stage manager is one who "has charge of everything backstage." This is literally true. However, the stage manager is more than a foreman in charge of the producer's backstage employees.

While the designer, playwright, and director are engaged in the realm of ideas, in creative work, and the actors and other backstage employees are engaged in interpretive or purely functional activities, the stage manager's duties lie between these two branches of the production team. He is a link between ideas and actualities.

Although he is a member of Actors' Equity and is bound and protected by the Equity contract, he is not an actor. As an individual the stage manager may be highly skilled in any one or several branches of the theater—acting, directing, lighting—but while he is a stage manager he functions as a liaison between all production departments.

The source of inspiration for any production is the playwright's manuscript. That is basic. Also, in producing a play, there is someone whose spark gives life and design to the production. This giver-of-the-spark, this animator or inspiriter, may be the producer; or the director, playwright, or the production's star. The reader is reminded of this rather obvious fact because he should not misunderstand when this handbook says the stage manager is the center of a production. The stage manager is, but not in the sense that he is the "spark." He is the center of a production because he deals with all members of the production staff, and because most elements of the production pass through his hands.

There have been various titles applied to the position the stage manager occupies. These titles have led to some confusion. They also have led to different, and sometimes erroneous, explanations of the stage manager's duties. Some textbooks on the theater have described him as the director's assistant, or a head technician, and let it go at that. In some cases and under certain circumstances, he may be the assistant director or a technician. In most productions he is not.

As the stage manager's position in all productions is not the same as that of a director's or producer's or star's assistant, it is inaccurate to approach his duties from the direction of any single staff member. The duties of the stage manager must be viewed in the light of all the other staff members' duties. The actual title given the stage manager's position is unimportant. The important thing is that whoever is in the position realizes that he is required to be the liaison for all staff members, with special emphasis being put on his work as "assistant inspiriter." The majority of men and women in New York who occupy this position prefer the simple title "stage manager."

A glance at the personnel in the unions of the theater will help the reader orientate himself as a stage manager among the other people in the profession. A chart of all the associated unions would be confusing and unnecessary. Such groups as many of the building-trade unions, ASCAP, television unions, the Inter-

INDEPENDENT ASSOCIATIONS

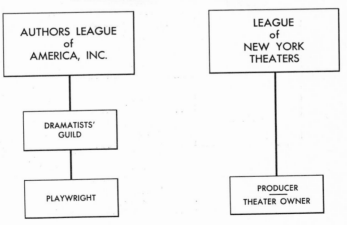

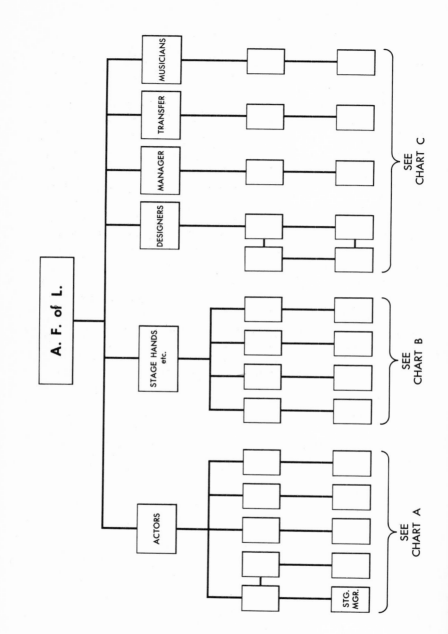

A. F. of L.

ASSOCIATED ACTORS and ARTISTES of AMERICA

ACTORS' EQUITY

CHORUS EQUITY

AMERICAN FEDERATION of RADIO ACTORS

AMERICAN GUILD of VARIETY ARTISTS

AMERICAN GUILD of MUSICAL ARTISTS

ACTOR
STAGE MGR.

MEMBER

MEMBER

MEMBER

MEMBER

CHART A

A. F. of L.

INTERNATIONAL ALLIANCE of THEATRICAL STAGE EMPLOYEES and MOTION PICTURE OPERATORS of the UNITED STATES and CANADA

THEATRICAL PROTECTIVE UNION LOCAL # 1	TREASURERS and TICKET SELLERS UNION LOCAL #751	THEATRICAL WARDROBE ATTENDANTS UNION LOCAL #764	DOORMAN'S UNION LOCAL #183
SCENERY, PROPERTY, LIGHTING & SOUND SHOP WORKMEN STAGE HANDS	BOX OFFICE TREASURERS	WARDROBE WOMEN DRESSERS	DOORMEN TICKET TAKERS USHERS

CHART B

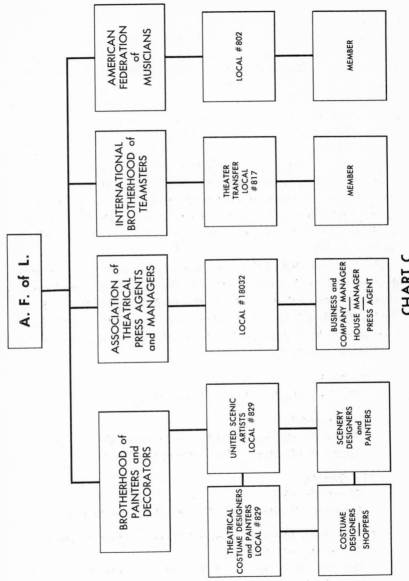

A. F. of L.

BROTHERHOOD of PAINTERS and DECORATORS

UNITED SCENIC ARTISTS LOCAL #829

THEATRICAL COSTUME DESIGNERS and PAINTERS LOCAL #829

SCENERY DESIGNERS and PAINTERS

COSTUME DESIGNERS SHOPPERS

ASSOCIATION of THEATRICAL PRESS AGENTS and MANAGERS

LOCAL #18032

BUSINESS and COMPANY MANAGER
HOUSE MANAGER
PRESS AGENT

INTERNATIONAL BROTHERHOOD of TEAMSTERS

THEATER TRANSFER LOCAL #817

MEMBER

AMERICAN FEDERATION of MUSICIANS

LOCAL #802

MEMBER

CHART C

national Ladies Garment Workers, and Sheet Metal Workers have not been included. The unions charted are those containing the majority of the workers a stage manager of a legitimate play meets in New York City. These charts should clarify questions about authority and jurisdiction.

Each union binds its members by laws and regulations which, in turn, govern the stage manager's actions. Some of the regulations will be met later in the handbook when they present problems to the stage manager, and will be discussed then. The union laws listed in Appendix D supplement and amplify those discussed in the handbook proper, and should give sufficient information for stage managers of most productions. If the stage manager meets regulations he does not understand, a consultation with the producer's general manager or the unions' business agents should set him straight.

The following list of the more important members of the production staff, with brief mention of the functions of each, will answer questions that may be in the reader's mind. The body of the handbook will furnish the stage manager's duties particularly as related to his liaison work between the other members of the production organization.

The Producer
The boss—he has charge of everything.

The Playwright
Writes the play and furnishes or approves all changes to it.
Approves all actors and sometimes the director.

The Director
Directs the play.
Approves all actors and all parts of the production.

The Business Manager (General Manager, Asst. Producer)
The producer's right hand.
Handles all financial details such as contracts, expenditures, budgets, etc.

The Designer(s)
Designs all settings, costumes, lighting, and properties for the approval of the producer, director, and playwright. Supervises the execution of his designs.

The Company Manager
The business manager's representative for a particular production especially at the theater and when on tour.

The Advance Agent
An advance publicity man for out-of-town tryouts and productions on tour.

The Publicity (Press) Agent
The New York publicity man. (Sometimes the same as the advance agent.)

Production Stage Crew:
Carpenter. Supervises original setup of scenery and, thereafter, is in charge of handling and maintenance of scenery. He is the traditional "head" of the production stage crew and, consequently, head man of all stage hands.

Property Man. Aids designer in procurement, collection, and preparation of properties. Thereafter in charge of their handling and maintenance.

Electrician. Aids designer by preparing and collecting lighting equipment, effects, and fixtures. Thereafter in charge of handling, maintenance, and operating lighting equipment.

Wardrobe Mistress. Aids designer in procurement, collection, and preparation of costumes. In charge of handling and maintaining them.

Sound Operator. Aids in procurement and collection of sound equipment and effects. Maintains and operates it.

Scenic Artist (Retouch Man)
A member of the scenic studio staff who retouches or repaints scenery in the theater.

Production Secretary

Often the director's private secretary, sometimes the manuscript typist.

Miscellaneous

The following personnel may be encountered; their titles explain their functions: Actor's Agent, Casting Director, Office Secretary, Office Typist, Accountant, Sound Technician, Orchestra Leader.

The production of a play may be likened to the manufacture of any complicated article. The various parts are created separately, are brought together at the proper time by careful planning and scheduling, and are assembled into a complete unit. After testing, the product is presented to the public.

The prerehearsal weeks and the first weeks of rehearsal are a period for planning and for starting the manufacture of the units of the production. The final rehearsal weeks see the beginning of assembling. During the setup and technical rehearsal periods the final assembling takes place. The dress rehearsal and tryout tour are the testing, and the New York opening is the presentation of the finished product to the public.

The parts of this handbook follow the development of the production of a play: the planning and creating of the units, the assembling, the testing, and the presentation to the public.

THE STAGE MANAGER'S HANDBOOK

PART ONE

Prerehearsal Period

THE MANUSCRIPT

The manuscript of a new play is its mainspring, the source of all ideas and activity. It will be one of the first things the stage manager meets in his new job, and from it he will determine his future action.

I. Filing and Recording. The stage manager is one of the first to come in contact with the manuscript of a new play. It will be his most important duty to preserve and expand this manuscript. As Actors' Equity does not permit a stage manager to work except at full salary, he often does not start work earlier than two weeks before the first rehearsal. This is what he will find: There will have been one or several "editions" of the play already typed and the copies scattered among the playwright, producer, director, designers, potential backers, and actors. Depending on the size of the producer's office staff, there may or may not be an accurate file record of the manuscripts. The stage manager should see that there is such a file, setting it up and keeping it himself if necessary. The file includes this information:

1. Copy identification—edition date and number
2. To whom issued and date

Each time sufficient changes in the manuscript are made to require fresh typing, a new "edition" comes into being. The first extant edition may be identified by "A" and the copies by "A1,"

1

"A2," "A3," "A4," "A5," "A6," starting with the top copy and going through the carbon copies in order of clarity. Most theatrical typists make six copies at a time, top and five carbons. The next edition will be "B," the next "C," and so on. Identifying numbers should be placed on the outside cover and title page of each copy.

In a large production involving many actors and staff members, it is an advantage to have the manuscript mimeographed. This is done only after the playwright, producer, and director agree that the manuscript is in a form that requires no further major change. Mimeographed editions come in lots of twenty-five or more copies and should be filed and recorded as accurately as other editions.

The stage manager should see that no replaced scene or portion of dialogue and stage direction is discarded or lost. As removed, these portions can be filed with identifying notes, such as, "Removed from Edition C, Act II, page 8, Oct. 10th." In time this may appear to be a collection of waste paper, but many occasions arise to justify its existence. Some playwrights insist that a copy of all discarded material be returned to them. Often it is decided to return to a version of a scene discarded weeks before. The stage manager is expected to have a copy. This collection of discards may be destroyed only after the New York opening of the play and then only after permission is received from both the playwright and the producer.

II. Editing and Typing. The stage manager must take care that the latest edition of the manuscript is in the hands of a typist in sufficient time for parts (sides) to be typed. These parts must be ready before the first rehearsal in time for the stage manager and his assistants to proofread them. This may be done by each manager checking several parts simultaneously while a reader goes straight through the play. The top (clearest typed) set of parts should be reserved for actual rehearsals. The other sets may be used for readings, understudies, and spares. Normally three sets of parts are received from the typist. Parts should be numbered and filed as accurately as manuscripts.

Some directors prefer that parts be typed without many of the stage directions furnished by the playwright. Entrances, exits, and other pertinent movements are included, but mood directions, elaborate stage directions, and scenery descriptions are not. The stage manager will edit the manuscript copy furnished the typist. If the stage directions are to be eliminated or minimized, it is useful to have the corrections made in the final edition of the complete manuscript before it is typed. This will save the stage manager many hours consumed by canceling out conflicting stage directions from the prompt script.

III. Planning the Performance Pattern. The ultimate goal of the professional theater is the presentation of a play before a paying audience. When the stage manager reads and studies the manuscript, he thinks in terms of the performance and the form it will assume. This form, this scheme for organizing and managing the performance, this shape or plan of what happens during the performance, is called the "performance pattern" in this handbook. If the play to be produced is one of Shakespeare's, the pattern will be considerably different from the pattern for *Abie's Irish Rose*. The stage manager, along with other members of the production staff, determines this pattern by a study of the manuscript.

The stage manager isolates, analyzes, and records the elements of the production. This process is called by some stage managers "breaking down the script." The elements of the breakdown are recorded in two main parts: (1) the plots, and (2) how to execute or activate the plots. The preliminary recording of the elements of the breakdown is also the start of the prompt script.

Since this prompt script eventually will be the heart of any production, care must be taken in its creation. The term "prompt script" is qualified by different people in different ways. The term "working prompt script" is often heard. This indicates that the speaker is referring to the stage manager's own script, which has been marked for use during the rehearsal or performance; while identical to other scripts in so far as dialogue is concerned, it will differ from them in many respects. The use of "prompt script" in this handbook will be all-inclusive. The reader should bear in mind that (a) the prompt script starts as a manuscript received from the playwright without plots or other technical details; (b) during rehearsals, try-outs, and up to opening night and sometimes thereafter, the prompt script undergoes constant revision, elaboration, and inclusion of technical details; (c) it is brought into a finished state after the opening. If the reader remembers this, he should have no difficulty identifying the nature of the prompt script as he progresses through this handbook.

Char-acters	ACT I		ACT II	ACT III
	Scene 1 Living Room	Scene 2 Bedroom	Hunting Lodge	Living Room
JOHN	Dinner Jacket	1. Pajamas 2. Suit	Tweeds	1. Dinner Jacket 2. Smoking "
MARY	Evening Gown	Nightgown & Robe	1. Traveling Suit 2. Slacks, Jacket	Evening Gown (Blue)
ANN (Maid)	Uniform (Black)	Uniform (Same?)		Uniform?
JEEVES (Butler)	Uniform			Uniform
etc.	etc.	etc.	etc.	etc.

When the stage manager is working from an early edition, he will do little physically to the manuscript. He will do the following:

    a) Read and reread the manuscript and become thoroughly familiar with it. Take particular note of technical difficulties—"impossible" situations—such as entrances from the wrong side, time discrepancies, and difficult costume changes.

b) Make preliminary plots:
1. Actor plot
2. Costume plot
3. Lighting plot
4. Sound plot
5. Property plot

c) Make a master cue sheet.

A. THE PLOTS. a) and b) *Actor and Costume Plot.* The preliminary actor plot should show the character's name and the scenes in which he appears. It can be combined with the preliminary costume plot, as illustrated on page 4.

At a glance this preliminary plot shows:
1. A list of the characters
2. In which scenes they appear
3. A general idea of the costuming involved

It also poses a few questions which must be answered eventually and serves to keep these questions in mind. In Act I, Scene 2, JOHN changes from pajamas to a business suit. Will this necessitate a quick-change room in the wings? Also, ANN appears in night and morning scenes. Does she wear the same uniform? In Act II, MARY changes from a traveling suit to slacks. Materials, color, and style do not concern the stage manager now, if ever, but it is his concern that MARY must make the change in privacy offstage in the time allotted by the covering dialogue. He must bring this problem to the attention of the playwright, director, scene designer, and costume designer, any one or all of whom may have overlooked it. At this point the stage manager need concern himself only with the physical requirements imposed by the manuscript.

c) *Lighting Plot.* The preliminary light plot (the "ing" in "lighting" is frequently dropped by theater people) may be very simple or fairly elaborate depending on the play, but, simple or not, should be outlined.

ACT I		ACT II	ACT III
Scene 1 Living Room	Scene 2 Bedroom	Hunting Lodge	Living Room
Evening – Table lamps are light source – possible fading of light outside window – no special effects	Morning – Bright morning sunlight from windows – no special effects.	Afternoon – Warm afternoon sun through windows – no change or effects	Night – Thunder storm – lightning outside window – table lamps flicker, brighten, go out – candles used temporarily (electric candles?) lights on dim – brighten – snap off individually – fireplace flicker thruout scene

Here again the stage manager is concerned with the finding of problems, not their solution. A stage manager rarely does the original lighting; the scene designer does, although the stage manager is frequently consulted about problems.

d) Sound Plot. The sound plot may be constructed in the same form as the light plot and should include all effects no matter how trivial with ample notes and descriptions of them.

From this preliminary plot the over-all requirements may be determined. Explicit dialogue for recordings will be supplied by the playwright and director.

e) Property Plot. The preliminary property plot need not be elaborately set up but should be as complete in detail as possible, including all properties that are described by the author either directly or indirectly in the stage directions or by the characters in their dialogue. Placement and arrangement of the properties will be added to the prop list before the setup and dress rehearsals. (See page 8.)

Bear in mind that these are *preliminary* plots, which will

ACT I		ACT II	ACT III
Scene 1	Scene 2		
Telephone bell (Supply 2 Sets)	NO EFFECTS	Automobile offstage approaching & stop, starting & leaving. (high-powered car) Voice calling in distance & echoing among hills (special recording?)	Thunder-all variations Practical telephone When used audience hears: Ringing at other end Busy signal Voices, male & female, not words
etc.		etc.	etc.

Specifications

1. Automobile associated with Stage R.
2. Echoing voice comes from "all around" - actors cannot determine where caller is.
3. Thunder "all around."
4. Intercom system for stage manager controlled from prompt desk with 5 stations as follows:
   - Station 1 - All stations hooked together
   - " 2 - O.P. (Opposite Prompt side)
   - " 3 - Upstage Center
   - " 4 - Fly floor or pin rail
   - " 5 - Switchboards
5. Special mike in foots leading to prompt desk to pick up cues (this may be extended to dressing rooms as monitor for actors).
6. Intercom between audience and switchboard for designer when lighting show.

etc.   etc.

undergo change and elaboration during rehearsals and will develop into finished plots after the play has opened.

B. THE MASTER CUE SHEET. *a) Activating the Plots.* The performance is built from many interdependent elements. Each element gets its origin from another and in turn acts as the source of still another element. Thus the whole performance is interlocked or keyed together. In the theater the source, the originating word or act, is known as a cue. Sometimes the complete action, the source and the result, the initiating force and its outcome, the cause and the effect, also is known as a cue, but is better called a "completed cue." The stage manager must see

ACT I, Scene 1
Living Room

SET PROPS (Heavy or fixed props)

Couch
Table (fairly large)
Table (bridge, folding)
Armchair (large, solid back, actor hides behind it)
Desk (special top - letter opener to be stuck into it)
Practical roller window shade on window D.R.
etc., etc.

SMALL PROPS (including décor when known, hand and personal props and
actor using them)

Cigarette lighter (JOHN)
Cigarette case (JOHN)
Tray of 6 cocktail glasses, martinis (BUTLER), actors never drink
Evening bag (Mary) , must have compartment for revolver - COSTUMES
Dial telephone handset on desk - practical – SOUND NOTE
etc., etc.

ACT,I, Scene 2
Bedroom

SET PROPS

Double bed, no footboard, reinforced three sides for sitting
Dressing table
Heavy drapes on window, practical draw type
etc., etc.

SMALL PROPS

Cigarette case (JOHN) conspicuously different from case Act I, Scene I
Hand mirror on dressing table – pink plastic – long handle
etc., etc.

ACTS II & III

etc.   etc.

that the elements are interlocked properly, that the cuing is
accurate.

The reader may wonder why cuing, primarily a performance
duty, is discussed in detail now. It must be realized that one of
the stage manager's most important functions is to anticipate. The
producer will expect his stage manager to foresee the problems of
how to accomplish the interlocking of the production elements,
and to solve the problems during this, the planning, period. Now
is the time to alter or adjust the production elements to fit into
the ultimate pattern, not later during the assembling and testing

periods when loss of time will be wasteful and expensive. The stage manager must study the manuscript thoroughly and develop a pattern of performance built upon interlocking cues.

Cues divide themselves easily into two types, direct and indirect.

1. *Direct Cues.* Most of the performance cues will be direct cues. Each word of dialogue is, in a sense, a cue for the succeeding word. An actor, waiting outside an entrance, hears another actor say a particular word; then the first actor enters. He has received a direct cue. An electrician watches an actor put his hand on a lamp switch, and then the electrician throws a switch supplying current to the lamp. The electrician has received a direct business cue. He also has received a "sight cue." These direct cues constitute the bulk of the play and will take care of themselves. The stage manager determines that the giver and receiver of the cue understand that it is a direct cue, stands by to assist if necessary, but can presume that, once learned, it will be accomplished automatically.

2. *Indirect Cues.* The stage manager will sort out from all the cues those that cannot be received automatically and directly. These will need an intermediary or relay to get the impulse from the source to the receiver. This relay is often the stage manager himself, or he is the supervising agent, overseeing personnel or mechanical relays.

To accomplish these indirect cues the stage manager will have two types of equipment, the fixed equipment found in the theater, and the special equipment that the stage manager devises and has the production furnish.

(1) *Fixed Equipment.* Every theater furnishes some permanent cuing equipment, usually built into the theater at the time of its construction. This equipment varies greatly in elaborateness and usefulness from theater to theater but generally includes: signals to the dressing rooms, signal to the stage hands' room, signal to the orchestra pit, signal to the orchestra greenroom, curtain signal, and lobby signal. The stage manager can expect to find these systems in varying forms and degrees of repair and

usefulness. All other necessary cuing devices will be planned by the stage manager and furnished by the production.

(2) *Portable (or Production-furnished) Equipment.* Of the cuing equipment that the production may furnish, personnel is the most important. By utilizing personnel to relay the cue, the stage manager eliminates the outstanding drawback to other cuing systems, mechanical failure. Personnel generally use voice or hand cues which consist of a warning, a ready, and a go. The warning should be given sufficiently in advance of the ready to allow the receiver time to make last-minute preparations. The ready and go come fairly close together. The warning may be given by voice or some other means. The arm raised over the head is the ready, and the arm dropped to the side is the go.

Buzzers and bells can be used but are confusing. They are useless during quiet scenes unless they sound in a remote part of the theater.

Light-cue systems usually consist of a pilot light and switch at the prompt desk, and a cue light at the point where the cue is to be received. The light on means ready; the light off means go. These light systems often are wired in series, a disadvantage, because a burned out pilot light means a dead cue light. Should this happen during the giving of a cue, confusion and error will result. Wiring the system in parallel, with two bulbs at the cue-receiving end, will eliminate this problem, since the chance of both bulbs burning out simultaneously is infinitesimal.

Increased efficiency has brought intercommunication systems more and more into favor as a means of giving cues and as a monitor in dressing rooms and corridors. Their advantages are several: the spoken word will attract attention when a light may not; interlocking systems allow the stage manager to give cues individually to distant stations or collectively to several or all stations (a flexibility most light systems do not have); in case of mishap the stage manager can carry on a conversation with distant points; and any one outlet can be used for various departments or functions by using a single introductory word such as "Props!" or "Actors!"

A microphone pickup in the footlights leading to a monitor on the prompt desk is valuable both in very quiet scenes and in scenes where there is a great deal of offstage noise.

Intercom systems have their drawbacks. Mechanical failure is an obvious one, and so there must be an alternate, independent system of some variety standing by. This may be a light system. In very quiet plays voice cues are dangerous and an intercom system is used sparingly. Monitors in dressing rooms may lead to indifference on the actor's part. One may become so familiar with the ticking and hourly striking of a clock that one ignores it. The same can happen with a monitor. Also, compared to a light system, an intercom system is expensive. This last point will interest the business manager.

b) *Composing the Cue Sheet.* After having studied the manuscript until he is thoroughly familiar with it, and having made the preliminary plots, the stage manager records how the elements will be activated. This record will be the preliminary master cue sheet. It has been seen that direct cues take care of themselves, and so this will be a listing of indirect cues.

A study of all preliminary plots and the master cue sheet will enable the stage manager to spot discrepancies and impossible situations, to plan the equipment needed for accomplishing cues, and to establish the basic performance pattern. Rehearsals, rewriting, and other factors will make changes and additions to the plots and cue sheets, but the basic pattern has been discovered.

The following excerpt from a playwright's manuscript will be used as the source material for the example of a master cue sheet:

(MARY turns off the overhead light, lowers the volume of the radio, and exits into the bedroom. In a moment the audience is aware that the elevator is in use. The elevator door opens, JOHN enters from the elevator, turns on the overhead lights, takes off his coat and hangs it in the closet. The elevator door has closed. JOHN turns off all lights and the radio and exits into the bedroom.)

PRELIMINARY MASTER CUE SHEET

(Departments are abbreviated : L for Lights, S for Sound, C for Carpenter, etc.)

Cue No.	Department Cue No.	C U E	Method
46	L-12	Overhead lights – OFF	Hand Signal
47	S-4	Radio volume – LOWER	Intercom
48	L-13	Elevator "In Use" pilot light - ON	Light Signal
49	L-14	Elevator lights thru translucent elevator door windows - UP (seen rising from downstairs)	Light Signal
50	C-4	Elevator door - OPEN	Hand Signal from Asst. Stg. Mgr.
51	L-15	Overhead lights – ON	Hand Signal
52	C-5	Elevator door – CLOSED	Hand Signal from Asst. Stg. Mgr.
53	L-16	"In Use" light – OFF	Light Signal
54	L-17	Overhead lights – OFF	Hand Signal
55	S-5	Radio volume – OFF	Intercom
56	L-18	Table lamp D.R. – OFF	Hand Signal
	etc.	etc. etc.	etc.

IV. Preparing Prompt Script for Rehearsals. During the weeks before the first rehearsal the manuscript will have been brought into a working edition by the playwright and director and usually is retyped. If the stage manager has been using an early edition for his preliminary work, he will abandon this early edition and will take the top copy of the latest edition for his prompt script and a good carbon copy for his assistant. If available, he should have a third copy as a reserve.

To be ready for the first rehearsal, the stage manager should make the following preparations to the manuscript:

a) Rebind the script. Remove the brass paper fasteners and insert the loose pages in a spring-backed, rigid binder. These binders are known to the stationery trade as "loose sheet holders." This protects the script with a sturdy cover, prevents dog-earing and tearing of pages, and forms a background on which to write when not at a table.

b) Insert opposite each page a sheet of 8½ × 11 typewriter paper (same size as manuscript). These sheets serve as a handy note pad, additional space for recording stage directions and inserted dialogue, etc. The sheets may be removed when prompting starts, for they may confuse the prompter.

c) Index the script with tabs, one for each scene. In a many-scene play individual scenes are often referred to by number—Act One, Scene 1 is 11 (eleven), Act One, Scene 2 is 12 (twelve), Act Two, Scene 1 is 21 (twenty-one), Act Three, Scene 1 is 31 (thirty-one), etc. Appropriate scene numbers should be put on the tabs.

d) Mark the cues and actors' entrances in the script. This may be done with pencils of different colored leads— possibly blue for actors' cues, red for sound, green for lights, brown for scenery and curtain cues.

At the beginning of each scene a list of actors in that scene should be made and can be divided as follows:

> *At Rise:*
> > Onstage: JOHN
> >   MARY
> > Ready Off: BUTLER
> >   MAID
> > *Later:*   POSTMAN
> >   MARTHA

At a glance it is evident that when the scene starts JOHN and MARY must be onstage. The BUTLER and MAID must be ready for immediate entrances in the order listed, and during the scene the POSTMAN and MARTHA will enter in that order.

It is customary to precede each cue by a warning, usually one or more minutes of dialogue or stage business before the actual cue. One manuscript page is approximately one minute. This warning is marked in the right margin of the manuscript and is in the color of the type of cue. E.g., "WARN POSTMAN" (in blue pencil) or "WARN PHONE" (in red pencil). A page or so later in the right margin opposite the cue word in the dialogue, which should be underscored, should be marked "POSTMAN" or "PHONE" in the appropriate color. A line drawn from the warning to the cue along the right margin will serve as a constant reminder that a cue is imminent. When a cue occurs at the top of a page a notation of some kind may be made on the preceding page so that the cue will not be missed while turning the page.

An attempt should be made to give warnings and cues, especially those that result in backstage movement and preparation, during audience laughs or action on the stage. E.g., call the stage hands onto the stage for a scene shift not only in sufficient time to prepare themselves but during a portion of the scene when the arrival backstage of ten or twenty people will not disturb the performance. No matter how careful they are, ten people cannot avoid making some noise.

e) Be sure to put the producer's and stage manager's names and addresses in the prompt script. Heaven help the stage manager who loses his script!

Having made the above preparations, the stage manager's script is ready for rehearsals. During rehearsals and tryout performances, changes and additions to the script will be made. There are as many different methods of accumulating, tabulating, organizing, and recording the material that will go into a prompt script as there are stage managers. Each stage manager will have his preferred system, but will find it necessary to alter it to fit the demands of a particular production. Whatever his system, the stage manager will keep in mind the elements a completed prompt script must contain, and will add them as they are developed during the rehearsal period.

The completed prompt script is not the manuscript as received from the playwright or the one the reading public gets from the publisher. The first is lacking in technical details, and the latter is elaborated with descriptive material to help the reader visualize the physical production and understand the written word. The finished prompt script is a record of a play's production elements, and it is a guide to a method of bringing those elements into existence on a stage. With the single exception of the playwright's dialogue, which is preserved accurately, the prompt script is not a literary achievement.

The finished prompt script contains:

a) *Introduction*
   1. Title Page
   2. Lists of Cast of Characters and the Scenes
   3. A copy of the opening night program
   4. A full-stage picture of each set or a small-scale ground plan of each set or both

b) *The Play*
   1. Complete dialogue
   2. Complete stage directions, including each actor's business, using traditional stage symbols or conventional abbreviations
   3. Short, instructive mood or character directions such as, "tearfully," "happily," etc. The playwright will amplify these for the reading public; the stage manager will not, except when the meaning is not self-evident in the context.

        4. Brief descriptions of the settings, including placement of important furniture, doors, windows, stairs, etc.

c) *The Technical Plots*

        1. Carpenter (Scenery) Plot includes types of scenery and how they are handled in the shifts

        2. Property Plot—a brief but complete identifying description of every property and its placement on- or offstage

        3. Lighting Plot—complete listing of all equipment and its placement and purpose. A list of all lighting cues

        4. Costume Plot—complete list in detail of all costumes for each actor, including accessories and unusual make-up

        5. Sound Plot—list of equipment, including records and effects and all cues

BUSINESS MANAGER AND STAGE MANAGER

One of the first members of the staff the stage manager meets is the producer's general business manager. This may be the producer himself. The business manager will help pave the way for appointments with the other staff members and will decide what firms the stage manager will deal with (typing agency, sound equipment company, etc.)

I. Production Schedule. Between them the business manager and stage manager will discuss the over-all production schedule, including:

        1. Date of first rehearsal

        2. Length of rehearsals (number of days)

        3. Places to rehearse. As these are limited, this schedule should be as complete as possible.

        4. Date and place of scenery setup. Does the studio constructing and painting the scenery make provision for the actors to see it in the studio before the stage setup?

        5. Date of technical rehearsals

        6. Date of dress rehearsals

7. Dates and places of out-of-town tryouts
8. When and where will photos of the actors in costume and in the settings be taken?
9. When will the production heads of the stage crews be hired? Who are they? An experienced stage manager's suggestions are appreciated.
10. When during the rehearsal period will it be possible to hire a property man so that props may be used?

II. Assistant Stage Managers. The selection of assistant stage managers is one of the first matters taken up between the business manager and the stage manager. The nature of the production is the deciding factor in the selection. Large scenery productions or small productions, many cues or few cues, number of actors, and type of actors (the assistant invariably understudies) are elements that help determine the number and type of assistants. A general but safe rule for determining number is: after the New York opening, the stage manager should be able to leave the backstage area and watch an entire performance from the audience with the assurance that the performance will be conducted efficiently during his absence. If he cannot do this, the production is understaffed or the stage manager has poorly trained assistants.

Many producers permit the stage manager to pick his own assistants, particularly if the production is heavy. This situation is ideal because assistants familiar with the stage manager's methods may be selected, subject only to the approval of director and playwright as to their suitability as small-part and/or understudy actors.

When the stage manager is unable to pick his own assistants, he should request that those picked for him be put on salary as soon as possible before rehearsals start. The stage manager not only requires their services but must learn their capacities before the pressure of rehearsals is upon them. The stage manager must divide his responsibilities. To do this he will find out which of his assistants is best equipped to manage cues, or actors, or costumes, or other production details. Furthermore, it is essential that more than one stage manager be familiar with *all* the details of the stage manager's part of the production. The production of a play must not be interrupted by the loss of the stage manager owing to sickness or any other reason. Once the assistants are hired, the stage manager will keep them posted on all details of his work. *No stage manager worth his salt withholds any pertinent information concerning the production from his assistants. He has no "trade secrets."*

III. Preparation of Rehearsal Stage Floor. The business manager may or may not have included in his budget provisions for hiring stage hands to mark the rehearsal stage with ground plans of the settings. This matter is taken up at this early time, because it may not be too late to make budget arrangements if the business manager agrees that it is necessary.

When a permanent place of rehearsal has been procured, arrangements can be made to mark the ground plans for the settings on the stage floor. If no permanent place is available a temporary ground cloth may be marked. This latter method has the advantage of mobility as the ground cloth may be moved to another place of rehearsal.

Some stage managers use narrow cloth tapes cut to the dimensions of the setting and thumbtack them to the stage floor. A different color for each setting is used. These tapes may be placed and removed quickly and be transported from one rehearsal hall to another easily.

The use of a ground cloth, permanent markings, or tapes involves hiring stage hands to lay the ground cloth and mark it, apply permanent markings, or lay out the tapes. This matter must be discussed with the business manager because he hires stage hands. If rehearsals are on a stage in a theater, the stage manager may not make elaborate, although temporary, chalk ground plans. A stage hand must be hired to do this also. A stage manager is permitted to make a *few* rough chalk marks to indicate essential doors, stairs, etc.

IV. Address List. It is important to get an address list started. This list should include the addresses and phone numbers of all persons connected with the production, including: actors selected, playwright, director, producer (home phone), business manager (home phone), producer's office, designers' and assistants' office and home phones, stage managers, publicity agent, company manager, crew heads, and any other specials. Most people prefer this to be a typed list on one sheet of paper that may be carried easily in the pocket. It should be dated and kept up-to-date. Copies should be given the producer, director, business manager, office secretary, company manager, each stage manager, each designer, publicity agent—but not given out indiscriminately, since the list often includes unlisted, private numbers. This list will grow and change daily and must be kept current. The business manager will furnish the material to *start* the address list; the stage manager will keep it current. The services of the office typist are enlisted when preparing an address list.

V. Sound Equipment. Utilizing the preliminary sound plot the business manager and stage manager will discuss sound equipment problems.

1. What effects are required?
2. Amount and type of equipment to be used
3. Intercommunication system for cuing
4. Intercommunication system from stage to dressing rooms
5. Special recordings to be made
6. Releases for standard recordings
7. Is a sound technician required? Who?
8. What firm will supply the equipment?
9. Has an operator been hired? Who?

VI. Music—Orchestras. A matter to settle relatively early is music. This is separate from recordings and includes music between the acts by an orchestra in the pit, live music on- or offstage, or a musician to play offstage while the actor "fakes" playing. This problem is usually put into the hands of a competent musician, who, with the playwright, producer, and director, selects the music and musicians. Sometimes the problem is left to the stage manager to settle. The business manager will advise the stage manager as to how the problem is being handled. Later the stage manager will discuss the matter with the designer when they plan cuing facilities and backstage arrangements.

DIRECTOR AND STAGE MANAGER

As soon as possible the stage manager consults with the director, and they discuss:

I. Rehearsal Schedule. The director will have his own method of directing. It is the job of the stage manager to adapt himself to it and help the director in every way. These methods vary greatly. Some directors plot a progress chart weeks in advance and manage to adhere to it. Others have an "Oh, we'll start by reading for a few days and then see what happens" method. The stage manager will be prepared to size up the situation immediately. One thing must not be forgotten. Time must be allotted for special rehearsals and performances for sound recordings or other "specials." With some directors this is no problem, but with a director who has no foreseeable plan, the stage manager must be an opportunist and seize time from the director to accomplish essential things. These latter directors are rare, fortunately. However, all people become absorbed in their work, and someone must have an eye on the clock to see that appointments are kept, that all work gets done. The stage manager is the timekeeper.

II. Casting. The director will advise the stage manager on what parts have been cast and what is the method for future casting. Stars, featured players and some small-part actors may have been signed or decided upon before the stage manager has been hired, and an actors' file of some sort will have been established.

A. Cast List. A cast list for quick reference can be plotted like this:

CHARACTER	ACTOR	ALTERNATES	UNDERSTUDY
JOHN	Henry Henry (Enright)	1. John Jones (Broder) 2. Sam Smith (Broder) 3. Will Wilson (Morris)	Hanff Gonff
MARY	Eliza Licer (M.C.A.)	1. Mattie Matson (Enright) 2. Betty Boop (Liebling) 3. Catty Call (Morris)	Merribelle Dimples
ANN (Maid) Understudy	Merribelle Dimples	1. Susan Sloop 2. Hannah Humph	Lucy McGrew
JEEVES (Butler) Understudy	Hanff Gonff	1. Harry Heil 2. Bernie Bernard (Morris)	Dave Brown
POSTMAN (Understudy & Asst. SM)	Dave Brown	1. Jack Green	Jack Green
etc.	etc.	etc.	etc.

The names of alternates appear in order of preference. The names in parentheses are the actors' agents, if any.

B. ACTORS FILE. The actors file varies greatly in different producers' offices. Often a separate file is established for each new production. In any event the stage manager will be expected to keep this file up-to-date or furnish the material to do so. Usually the actor's card is filed alphabetically under the character name for which he is considered. This information should be included on the card:

1. Actor's name, address, phone number
2. Actor's agent with notation whether or not agent is acting for him in *this* production
3. Experience and special talents
4. Part for which considered
5. Possible other parts or understudy for which suited
6. Date and comment on any reading and initials of those attending reading

The actors file includes a card for each actor considered for a part, not just interviewed but seriously considered, whether he has a reading or not. This is not the stupendous task that it appears to be at first glance. As pointed out before, by the time the stage manager comes on the scene, or the profession is aware that casting is being done, a large portion of the cast is set. This means that the stage manager, who may be assigned the responsibility of screening all prospects, has his work outlined for him in a definite pattern. The requirements of the handful of parts left to be filled will automatically exclude most applicants.

C. INTERVIEWING ACTORS. There are three basic tests of the applicant for an acting job:

1. External or physical qualifications
2. The applicant's technique
3. The caliber of the applicant's innate ability

These are not in the order of importance, but in the order of obviousness.

1. Certain requirements, such as sex, age, or a physical characteristic cannot be circumvented. The prospect's experience and ability will not help him if he cannot fill these obvious requirements.

2. The ideal actor would be the individual whose body and mind are under such perfect control that he could call on any one of a complete range of attributes, or any combination of them, in order to portray any characterization. There is no need to enter into a discussion of the reasons some actors never achieve this control. Suffice it to say that they do not. They limit their range to those attributes which are similar to their outstanding and most-cultivated personal traits. Consequently the parts they play are restricted in scope. In general terms, they "play their personalities," or they are "types."

The experienced interviewer is immediately aware of the applicant's outstanding traits, and, if these traits coincide with the attributes necessary for a particular characterization, there has been a fortunate meeting. However, unless the interviewer is thoroughly familiar with the applicant's work, he will not know whether or not these apparent traits are the only ones in the applicant's range. This must be determined before an applicant is rejected, or valuable acting material may be overlooked. A brief review of the parts the actor has played may indicate his acting range. However, unless the interviewer has knowledge of the caliber of the companies with which the actor performed, and also has an exhaustive familiarity with plays of all ages and types, a review of the actor's career is of little help.

Sometimes a more satisfactory and accurate examination of the prospect may be made by having him give a reading from the manuscript.

If the interviewer feels that the prospect is capable of a characterization, he should refer the prospect to the producer and director. If he is certain that the prospect cannot do the job, he should tell him so immediately.

It is at this stage of casting that the difference between adequate casting and exceptional casting is determined. Casting that stops with the use of the obvious personality may be adequate, but it is rarely exceptional. Casting that digs out latent, unknown, or unused ability, ability that is not obvious, may develop exceptional results.

3. There have been many terms used in evaluating an actor's caliber. Some of them have been graphic. An actor of fine caliber "has it," or has "oomph," or "sends one." If his caliber is poor, he "leaves you cold." The use of these words is colorful, but too frequently they are adopted by inexperienced persons and, through misuse, lose their color and meaning. The conscientious casting interviewer will want more than general knowledge of the quality that determines caliber in an actor. Also he will want a yardstick by which he can measure his own ability as a judge. The psychologists have a word that helps. The word is empathy.

A thing (a voice, a color, any "thing") can induce an emotion. Empathy is the imaginative process that endows the thing with the emotion the thing has induced in the receiver. For example, a marble statue may induce in an observer sensations of coolness, serenity, and happiness. If the observer, by imaginative projection, endows the statue with these qualities, the statue itself (to the observer) becomes cool, serene, and happy. This imaginative process is empathy.

All individuals have the power or quality that generates this imaginative process in an observer or listener. Some have the power to a large degree and consequently can reach and influence a large number of receivers. Others have the quality to a lesser degree. This power, this quality, is frequently called empathic appeal. Those who have empathic appeal in large quantities can be found everywhere. They may be a butcher, baker, or housewife—they do not have to be in some branch of what is called entertainment. Quite often they do not consciously recognize that they have such appeal, or that they have put in motion the empathic process. However, to be an actor, one *must* have empathic appeal to a large degree, and one must be conscious of it and capable of utilizing it to generate the proper stimuli.

In the theater empathy, or the empathic process, has two important partners, the actor and the receiver, without whom there can be no process. The actor, with his empathic appeal, generates the stimulus. The receiver accepts the stimulus in the form of emotions, and imaginatively projects them back into the actor and endows the actor with them. Consequently the caliber of both actor and receiver determines the completeness and effectiveness of the empathic process. An actor with limited empathic appeal will generate correspondingly fewer and less powerful stimuli than an actor with great appeal. Also, an actor with great appeal may be ineffective to a poorly conditioned receiver. As the casting interviewer is a receiver, he must be prepared to recognize empathic-appeal caliber. By looking deeply into his own conditioning, he makes certain that he is prepared.

It can be seen that any person who approaches the problems of casting a play should do so with considerable forethought and caution. A stage manager, entrusted with the job of interviewing actors, will need infinite patience, ingenuity, imagination, experience, theater background, and personal discipline. He must constantly examine and evaluate his own, as well as the public's, receptivity to empathic appeal. And he must know how to recognize this appeal in actors who have not as yet learned to control it and present it with facility.

The actual mechanics of the interview are simple, if the interviewer is prepared. The only proper treatment of applicants is honesty. Those that obviously are not suited for a part should be told so immediately. Most actors appreciate such frankness. A file card need not be made for these rejects, but a record of the interview is valuable. Those actors that fall within the proper categories should be interviewed briefly and to the point: get name, address, agent, experience, and make a few identifying notes. Then tell them the truth, which is usually: their names are being taken for reference only; the producer is considering others; they may or may not be given an interview or reading with the director and producer; in the meantime they should not turn down any opportunity for other employment; the failure to get a part in this play does not militate against getting a part in a future production.

At first glance this may appear to be a form of "run-around." It is not. In addition to each actor settled upon for a part, the producer will want at least three alternates available. Thus, at least four possible applicants are needed. Common sense tells the stage manager that he cannot score perfectly each time with his first four choices. He must have a larger group from which the producer can make a selection. If out of fifteen to twenty "possibles" four finalists can be selected, the score is above average. The actor should understand that he is on a "possible" list and that his chance for a part is—and this is a highly optimistic figure —no better than one in twenty. When the actor knows this, he will understand that he is not "getting a run-around."

Once in a while an actor especially right for a part will come along. Try to have the producer and director furnish a schedule of times when they are available to see applicants, so that the applicant may be given a definite appointment then and there. Take more copious notes on this actor, and add them to his file card. The cards of the applicants can be given to the producer and director before they have the interviews. This helps the interviewer prepare for a more thorough and satisfactory interview.

D. TRYOUTS AND READINGS. The terms "reading" and "tryout" are used by most people interchangeably. The purist will use "reading" to indicate a test of the actor by means of the dialogue. "Tryout" will indicate something physical, such as an ability to dance, sing, play the trombone, or stand on one's head. Very often the test of the actor will include elements of both readings and tryouts. This handbook uses the term "reading" most of the time, but the reader may substitute "tryout" if he wishes, as the methods of conducting both are fundamentally the same.

Tryouts or readings should be reduced to a minimum when possible. As noted before, in the average cast many of the parts will have been filled before the stage manager is hired. This leaves only a few readings necessary, but even these must be kept to a minimum and handled with dispatch. In most cases the producer and director will have a preferred or established system for handling these readings and will outline it to the stage manager. Sometimes they rely on the stage manager to devise a system. In any event it will devolve on the stage manager to organize the details and make the system function.

The stage manager should be acquainted with an Equity rule concerning readings. The prospect reads only with the director or the stage manager, or their assistants. The producer does not have two prospects read together, except with the following understanding. Should two prospects read together, even though one be the star who has already been hired, the prospects may hold the management to a two-week standard minimum contract.

Readings will necessarily include the playwright, the producer, and director, since their approval must be obtained for all casting. Others included may be the production's star, the stage managers, the actor's agent, and the business manager. It is best to keep the number of participants small. Some readings are held in the producer's office or apartment, where a relaxed and cozy atmosphere presumably exists. These *in camera* readings usually employ only the playwright, producer, director, and prospect. Other readings are quite formal and are held on a stage. Still others take place in a noisy corridor! Wherever held, the following preparations should be made:

a) The actor and his agent should be notified well in advance to prepare for the reading. This includes an opportunity for the actor to familiarize himself with the scene to be read.

b) The scenes to be read by each character should be decided beforehand, and sufficient copies of the manuscript or special copies of the scene should be on hand. Parts may be used but are less satisfactory than scenes containing the complete dialogue.

Specially edited copies of a scene are useful, because an emphasis may be placed on the lines the prospect will read. Intervening lines by other characters may be shortened or eliminated. Thus a flow or continuity may be given the prospect's dialogue that isn't there in the complete manuscript. These scenes are prepared after permission is received from the playwright and director.

c) A typed schedule of appointments should be on hand for all. This schedule should include:

1. Date and time
2. Actor's name, agent, part for which considered
3. Space for notes and comments

As soon as possible after the reading a decision should be made and reported to the actor or his agent. This reporting often is left to the stage manager and takes one of three forms:

a) Yes—the actor is hired.

b) No—the actor is not to be hired.

c) Perhaps—the actor is being considered along with several others, and a decision will be reached by next Tuesday.

A yes or no report should be given whenever possible. Stalling an actor or keeping him on tenterhooks can be very upsetting as well as financially disastrous, if he turns down other employment because of indecision. The stage manager should keep a record of actors being kept in abeyance and should try to get decisions about them made as soon as possible. After a reading a note of its outcome should be made on the actor's file card.

To repeat, the number and length of readings should be kept small. Readings and tryouts are very fatiguing for the listeners, and a tired judge is unfair to the actor and to the production.

E. UNDERSTUDIES. The producer, director, and playwright select the understudies; but, as the understudy setup may be complicated, the services of the business manager and stage manager are recruited. Also the business manager handles the actors' contracts and must include in them the exact parts an actor is to understudy, and the salary he receives if he should play a part.

The following understudy situation should be avoided. The letters represent the actors in the company and the understudies who cover them.

A, B, C, D, E, F, G, H, J, X, Y, Z, Asst. Stg. Mgr.

A)
C)   covered by   E

B)
D)   covered by   G
F)

E)
G)   covered by   H

H)
J)   covered by   X

X)
Y)   covered by   Asst. Stg. Mgr.
Z)

If Actor C cannot perform he is replaced by Actor E and a chain of replacements follows ending with an acting company in this sequence (replacements in quotes):

A, B, "E," D, "H," F, G, "X," J, "Asst. Stg. Mgr.," Y, Z.

Four replacements necessary to adjust for one absence!

The following method of understuding is more satisfactory:

A)
B)
D)   covered by   X
E)

C)
F)   covered by   Y
G)

X)
Y)   covered by   Asst. Stg. Mgr.
Z)

No matter which one actor is missing now, no more than two understudies will be used.

If more than one actor is absent, complications arise and lead to an elaboration often utilized. This is sometimes called "double-cover" and works like this: (Note that the stage manager is used. This is permitted by Equity for but one or two performances and then only when it is a double-cover. If the actors' absences are to be longer, a new actor or understudy must be hired.)

		1st Cover	*2nd Cover*
A)			
B)			
D)	covered by	X	Z
E)			
C)			
F)			
G)	covered by	Y	Asst. Stg. Mgr.
H)			
J)			
X)			
Y)	covered by	Asst. Stg. Mgr.	Stage Manager
Z)			

With this type of understudy schedule it is seen that, when Actors B and D are absent, the parts are covered by X and Z, and the company appears as follows:

A, "X," "Z," E, C, F, G, H, J, "Asst. Stg. Mgr.," Y, "Stg. Mgr." Not ideal, to be sure, but far better than losing a performance.

Very often a situation occurs in which no member of a company or the assistant stage manager is suitable as understudy for a part. E.g., in a company composed of middle-aged characters and a child no member of the company can understudy the child. In this case another child will be hired. This nonpart-holding, nonappearing understudy is known as a "walking understudy."

The system of understudying for a particular production may involve a combination of several methods. It can be seen that establishing the system will take careful planning. Whatever plan is decided upon, it is essential that understudies be hired as soon as the actors, for they must attend all rehearsals. They receive the benefit of the director's work with the regular actors, are available to stand in during rehearsals, and are prepared to go on even at dress rehearsals or openings. It is the duty of the stage manager to see that they are prepared.

Most producers look upon understudies as a form of insurance not unlike the more obvious fire and theft insurance, and are willing to pay weekly "premiums" for this insurance in the form of small additions to an actor's salary. This is arranged by the business manager at the time actors' contracts are signed. The stage manager cannot expect the actor to assume more understudy work than he has contracted for.

In general the use of understudies is an emergency measure, and most managements have a sensible attitude toward their use. The tradition that the show must go on is strong, but no show must go on using an actor if that actor will endanger his health. Managements will prefer that an actor lose several performances and thus prevent serious illness rather than continue to perform and eventually lose weeks of performance. Also, the chance of infecting the other members of the company cannot be ignored. With insurance, Blue Cross, drugs that shorten sickness, and other aids, the bugbear of lost income is not the serious problem to the actor that it was ten years ago. In most cases the management does not dock the actor's salary when he misses a few performances because of sickness.

With the above in mind, no actor should arrive at the theater too sick to perform. If he arrives at the theater at all, the management has the right to presume he is capable of going on. Should the actor find himself ill during the day, he should advise the management. This will give the stage manager, the understudy, and actors a chance to prepare for the sick actor's absence. And so, in most cases, discussions in this handbook concern themselves with absences and the use of understudies that arise from sudden illness or accident.

DESIGNER AND STAGE MANAGER

I. First Conference. In the early prerehearsal days the stage manager should arrange a meeting with the scene designer. As his most frequent contacts will be with the designer's assistants, he should meet them also as soon as possible. This will be a get-acquainted meeting primarily, but the following should be accomplished:

a) Get a floor plan of each set.

b) Study and thoroughly understand each set, using the scale models for study. Before and during rehearsals questions such as, "Is there room on this wall for a mirror?" "Which way does this door swing?" etc. will be asked. The stage manager must have the answers ready.

c) Turn over a copy of the preliminary plots to the designer. He undoubtedly will have more elaborate plots of his own, but a cross-check is essential. Discuss the lighting particularly.

d) Discuss the position of the prompt desk in relation to the scenery. This will entail a discussion of cuing facilities and should be as thorough as possible.

e) Discuss the building and placement of quick-change rooms in the wings, and other specials.

f) Arrange with the designer a time for a daily exchange of information. It should be understood that one of the functions of the designer is the design and procurement of properties. As the list of properties, as well as other elements of the production, will undergo change and elaboration during the rehearsal period, it is essential that the designer be apprised of changes promptly. He cannot be in attendance at all rehearsals. To accomplish this there should be a daily meeting, in person or over the phone, between the designer or his assistants and the stage manager. In this handbook this meeting is called an "Information Exchange."

In his position as liaison staff member, the stage manager must be prepared to do a certain amount of shopping or selection of properties and other production elements. He is often the only staff member, other than the director, who has exact knowledge of what is needed. Normally this information can be conveyed to the designer during the Information Exchange, but, to save valuable time, the stage manager may help make the actual selection. In these instances, the stage manager works in conjunction with the designer. The designer passes on the element's appropriateness in matters of taste, the stage manager in matters of practicability.

g) Determine what the designer will require while lighting the show, e.g., intercom set, etc.

II. Lighting Conference. The production electrician is selected as soon as possible by the business manager, designer, and sometimes the stage manager. The electrician will assist the designer select, prepare, and adapt the lighting equipment while working in the shop which will furnish the equipment. He may help manufacture special effects and other equipment.

The designer, stage manager, and electrician should have a conference at which the designer will outline his plan for the lighting of the production. This is discussed thoroughly. This very essential meeting eliminates or forestalls many future problems. The stage manager will furnish a cuing layout at this conference, especially any light-cue system that the electrician will furnish or prepare.

PUBLICITY AGENT AND STAGE MANAGER

The publicity agent will enlist the services of the stage manager in having the actors fill out publicity information blanks, making and keeping appointments, etc. The publicity man is not passing the buck in this matter. On the contrary, the stage manager should insist on handling these things, because, by doing so, he can prevent interrupting and wasting valuable rehearsal time. The stage manager does not initiate publicity appointments and the like, but he should screen and co-ordinate them.

COMPANY MANAGER AND STAGE MANAGER

The company manager is really an assistant business manager, and many of the stage manager's contacts with him will be the same as those with the general business manager. However, they will work closely on such matters as having the actors fill out tax-withholding blanks, social security blanks, etc. in order not to waste rehearsal time.

CONFERENCES

It must not be construed from the foregoing that the conferences listed comprise all the conferences the stage manager will attend. These are merely the ones he must initiate himself. He should attend all conferences, because, in his role as the liaison staff member, he must know practically all details of the production if he is to accomplish his liaison work intelligently.

THE STAR AND THE STAGE MANAGER

The stage manager usually meets the star many days before rehearsals start. He should be aware of the traditions governing his and other personnel's treatment of the star. Courtesy is as necessary in the theater as anywhere else. Unfortunately a newcomer may misinterpret these courtesies for sycophancy in the giver and for arrogance in the receiver.

The recruit in the army soon learns that military courtesy, demanding that he stand at attention when being addressed by a superior, is more than "respect for rank." It is also an indication that the soldier is conscious of the things inherent in the word "attention": readiness, alertness, industry, and an awareness that time cannot be wasted. In a like manner the courtesies given in the theater to the star, and in turn accepted and expected by him, are in actuality a form of insurance against wasting time and energy.

In the limited rehearsal period, the star has much more to accomplish than other members of the company. The star will have more dialogue to learn, more costumes to fit, more appointments to meet, will spend more time on stage, and so on. It is a matter of simple economics that this individual must be given every aid to accomplish a maximum of work with a minimum of effort, so that strength may be preserved and health safeguarded. If approached with this understanding in mind, it will be seen that "privileges of the star" are not added niceties or the trappings of pomp but very important adjuncts to the production.

When schedules are being made or appointments decided, it is customary to consult the star in advance. Help in obtaining transportation to and from rehearsals, seclusion for study when not needed at rehearsal, a close watch for fatigue, promptness on everyone's part, tailoring rehearsal lights, heat, and such things to best fit the star's well-being are among the many courtesies that may be extended.

If the star finds it necessary to demand courtesies, a close look into the root of the demand usually finds it is not a protest against an imaginary indignity or *lèse-majesté* but a sincere disapproval of waste and bad management. The same roots often underlie "temperamental outbursts."

It will be the responsibility of the stage manager to see that traditional courtesies are extended to the star, the hardest-working member of the company. This may mean explaining the reasons behind these courtesies to inexperienced personnel, and, unfortunately, may mean *demanding* courtesy from thoughtless and inconsiderate persons.

PREPARATION FOR THE FIRST REHEARSAL

Check List

1. Do the actors and understudies required for the first rehearsal (this may not be *all* actors) know the time and place of the first rehearsal?
2. Have all actors and understudies their parts?
3. Has Actors' Equity been advised of time and place of first rehearsal?
4. Has a list of all actors, including understudies and stage managers, been prepared ready to hand the Equity representative when he appears?

5. Has the rehearsal hall been checked well in advance of the rehearsal for:
   a) Size?
   b) Lights?
   c) Heat?
   d) Adequate tables, chairs, and ashtrays, enough for both setting the scene and the use of actors who are waiting?
   e) Smoking rules and facilities?
   f) Drinking water?
   g) Toilets?
   h) Are phones available? Has the office the numbers?
   i) Is there an attendant at the rehearsal hall? Does he know about the rehearsal?
6. Are ground plans and models of all sets available?
7. Are there extra manuscripts and parts immediately available?
8. Is there a supply of paper and pencils on hand?
9. Has a daily attendance chart been made to record the rehearsal hours of each actor, individually and in detail?
10. Do the producer, director, playwright, scene and other designers, and publicity agent know the time and place of the rehearsal?
11. Has the stage floor been marked with the ground plan?
12. Has the stage manager familiarized himself with Actors' Equity and other union rules concerning rehearsals?
13. Have the stage managers a pocketful of nickels and dimes for phone calls?
14. Is the prompt script prepared?

STAGE MANAGER'S EQUIPMENT

Mention should be made of equipment the stage manager will need. Over a period of years many stage managers accumulate a good deal which they find useful, particularly during tryouts and road tours, and it will be listed later. They use this equipment during rehearsals and New York runs because they have it, not because it is absolutely essential. There are things, however, the stage manager is expected to have.

1. A brief case of some sort
2. Dozens (literally) of sharpened pencils with erasers and some means of keeping them sharpened
3. Scratch pads
4. A clipboard—invaluable for note-taking and keeping plots, appointments, etc. handy
5. A measure of some sort, preferably two: a 12" ruler and a 6' folding rule or 25' cloth tape
6. Chalk
7. A watch and possibly a stop watch. The stop watch should be of the "sports timer" variety which allows starting, stopping, and resuming without resetting. This permits the stage manager to keep accurate record of the playing time even when there are many interruptions (times-out). Early in rehearsals the stage manager will want to time certain scenes, particularly cover scenes for costume changes and the like, and will report his findings to the director.

All the above, along with manuscripts and parts, ground plans, etc., can be carried in the brief case and should be sufficient to get rehearsals started. Many stage managers find a typewriter indispensable. Others get along without one, using office machines when necessary. The stage manager's equipment, like the sidewalk pitchman's, should be easily assembled and portable.

PART TWO

Rehearsals, First Weeks

The rehearsal period is short and consequently a time of great activity and intense concentration. The stage manager must see that time is not wasted. If he has a well-planned daily schedule, he is at an advantage. This schedule will be flexible to adjust to changes made by the producer and director; but, as certain things must be accomplished each day, it is wise to have them clearly in mind.

DAILY PREPARATION

I. Before Going to Rehearsal. Contact the office for last-minute advices. As the office may not open until approximately the same time that rehearsals start, it often is impossible for the stage manager to go personally to the office, and so contact may be made by phone.

II. At Rehearsal Hall. Be at rehearsal early to:
1. Advise office of phone numbers. The hall may not have been used previously, and the office will want to know how to make contact during the rehearsals.
2. Check light, heat, etc.
3. Prepare stage for rehearsal, including:
   a) If using a marked ground cloth, is it in place? Are tapes or chalk marks for proper set?

b) Is the proper furniture in place?

c) Are necessary rehearsal props available?

4. Check in actors, using "attendance record chart." This chart must be kept accurately. From it will be determined the first day of rehearsal for each actor, end of probationary period for each actor, exact time of each rehearsal, and rehearsal salary due each actor.

5. Transfer manuscript changes that have been received after the last rehearsal into actors' scripts.

6. Assign appointments for costume fittings, publicity, etc. These can be on separate reminder slips to hand the actor.

7. If another rehearsal hall is to be used in the future, have arrangements been made to transfer the ground cloth, rehearsal props, etc.?

8. Make final check with director before rehearsals start:

a) Acquaint him with appointments. He will have approved them before they are set, but he should be reminded.

b) Remind him of the status of actors on probation. The first five rehearsal days are a probationary period for each actor. If the actor is to be released, he must be so advised, *in writing, before* the cast is dismissed the fifth day of the actor's rehearsal. As all actors do not necessarily start rehearsing the same day, the probationary period for all actors is rarely the same. An accurate record must be kept of the first day each actor is called for rehearsal. This is done by the stage manager on the attendance record chart, as noted.

c) Establish the time the noon (or meal) recess will occur. Also the reconvening time and when rehearsals will be over for the day.

THE REHEARSAL

As a part of the first rehearsal, but before rehearsing or reading starts, the stage manager, in the presence of a representative of Actors' Equity, will read Equity rules to the company. Thereafter the stage manager is required to see that the rules are posted at the rehearsal hall during all rehearsals.

It will be essential for the stage managers to divide their work. As the prompt script is a full-time job for the stage manager, the assistant stage managers take over most of the other stage managerial rehearsal duties.

I. Rehearsal Duties of Assistants. The stage manager departmentalizes the duties of his assistants. A division of work might be as follows:

Asst. A
1. Actors:
 Check their attendance.
 Check their entrances and exits.
 Keep actors available. This does not mean "tying them to the stage," but no actor should leave the immediate vicinity without permission from the stage manager.
2. Properties:
 Arrange rehearsal furniture.
 Prepare rehearsal hand props.

Asst. B
1. Costumes:
 Record costume plot changes.
 Co-ordinate appointments for fittings, etc.
2. Handle all appointments.
3. Handle publicity forms, tax forms, etc.

Together—the assistants will:
1. Answer all phone calls and take messages.
2. Maintain quiet and order.
 a) It cannot be overemphasized that rehearsal days are few, the hours limited, and, consequently, a period

of concentration requiring a minimum of waste. The director's method will dictate the conduct of the stage managers, and they must do everything they can to ease the director's burden. If the director has not made clear his wishes before rehearsals, alert stage managers will soon determine them.

b) Movement or sound is distracting. Have actors not engaged in a scene wait as far offstage and downstage in the wings as possible, not upstage where they are in the director's line of vision. If actors enter from different sides of the stage, try to have them on the proper side before starting the scene, thus avoiding distracting crossings and recrossings of the stage.

c) The director usually prefers to be alone in the auditorium. Keep actors and all others out.

d) Shut all doors leading to the rehearsal area.

e) Advise doorman of rehearsal hours and names of the cast. He can be very useful in turning away unwanted visitors.

f) Muffle phone bells if necessary.

g) Rehearsal lights are notoriously bad. Endeavor to eliminate glare, and restrict bright light to the acting area.

h) Actors will adjust themselves to a routine and to an established personnel. Keep visitors away unless you can announce to all that they are expected. Make sure that the cast meets new actors joining the company.

3. Protect rehearsal hall property. It is rare these days to rehearse in an empty theater. Usually there is a show in residence. All properties, scenery, costumes, etc. of the incumbent must be left alone. Nothing may be used at any time for any purpose unless permission is received from the resident show's producer. Especial care must be taken

during wet weather. Umbrellas, galoshes, wet clothing, etc. can be very destructive. SMOKING RULES MUST BE ENFORCED.

II. Stage Manager's Duties. The stage manager prefers to handle the prompt script and related matters himself. He will watch the direction carefully, recording in the script all stage business, dialogue changes, and pertinent directions given. He will make notes on all props, costumes, lights, sound, etc. that are "created" or discussed during the rehearsal.

The stage manager usually works at a table placed near the footlights at one side of the stage beside the proscenium arch, where he can have an unobstructed view of the stage and the director in the auditorium. He chooses the side where his prompt desk will ultimately be when the scenery is used. Thus the actors may get accustomed to finding him in the same place.

A. TAKING NOTES. A convenient method of recording notes is to keep a sheet of paper handy on which columns with the following headings have been ruled:

Director	Mgr.	Designer	Costumes	Lights	Props	Misc.

Should any staff member appear at the rehearsal, a quick glance will suffice to find out if there are notes for him.

B. RECORDING STAGE DIRECTIONS. The markings, abbreviations, and symbols used in a prompt script to record action, emotion, tempo, and other elements are a type of shorthand and vary from stage manager to stage manager. There are certain traditional symbols that all theater people use. Standard stage-area abbreviations are indicated on the following chart. U. means Upstage, D. is Downstage, R. is Rightstage, L. is Leftstage, and C. is Centerstage. Thus U.R. is Upstage Rightstage, or more commonly, Up Right. D.L.C. is Down Left Center.

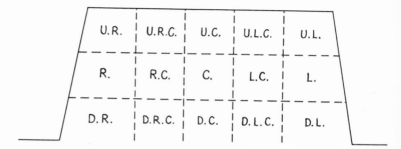

The above fifteen stage-area abbreviations normally suffice for the actors' onstage positions. Furniture or parts of the scenery are helpful locators. For example: "at window," "R. of table," "in doorway," or "on 3rd step" locate an actor immediately.

The letter X is frequently used to indicate a stage movement or cross. "X D.R." means "Cross to Down Right area." Small diagrams with arrows help clarify complicated movements.

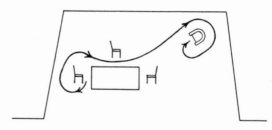

Complicated seating or other arrangements may be dia-grammed. Initials signify characters' names.

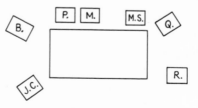

Recording characterization, emotion, and tempo is more difficult. The stage manager will want an accurate record of these
elements for two reasons. First, the producer expects to find them
in the prompt script, and second, they are invaluable as references
when checking performances months later. The stage manager
does not indulge in flights of description when recording. Suc-
cinctness is essential. By attending closely to all directions, all
discussions of characterization, emotion, and meaning, the stage
manager can spot several words or a short phrase that will sum
up the complete discussion. These are the words he records. With
a little practice and experience he will find that he will choose
the words that serve as a cue to remind him of the complete
direction or discussion. He records characterization, interpretation, and emotion in this manner.

Recording tempo imposes still another problem. Some stage
managers find the signs used in written music valuable for this
purpose. Crescendo and diminuendo signs may indicate tempo
and volume changes; rest signs of different types may indicate
pauses of various lengths. Another method of indicating pauses
is to insert a vertical line between words where the pause occurs.
Additional parallel vertical lines between the words may be
added for longer pauses. Each line can indicate a pause of one
"count," or approximately one second. Underscoring, bracketing,
dashes, and so on may also be used.

Various characteristics of speech, such as inflection, dialect,
and pronunciation, may be recorded by using accent marks,
underscoring, dashes, and phonetic symbols.

Those stage managers familiar with shorthand (Gregg, Pit-
man, or Speedwriting) often use shorthand characters for quick
recording. Incidentally, a knowledge of shorthand will be useful
to the stage manager at all times. Some words and marks used
in proofreading—delete, stet, $\wedge$ (insert), tr or $\cup$ (transpose),
etc.—are valuable. All methods, all abbreviations and symbols,
well-known or personal, must be transcribed by the stage manager into plain, simple language at the first opportunity.

C. ANSWERING QUESTIONS. Among the duties the stage manager is most frequently called on to perform is answering questions. As preparing and holding the prompt script will require his undivided attention most of the time, the stage manager should train actors and other backstage personnel not to disturb him when he is working. Most questions can be answered by the assistant stage managers, if the stage manager has shared his knowledge of production details with them. Therefore, questions should be addressed to the assistants first. If it is absolutely necessary to disturb the stage manager, personnel can be trained to approach the stage manager, get his attention without speaking to him, and wait until the stage manager may divide his attention at a time when doing so will not interfere with his job. Establishing this habit early in rehearsals is very valuable, as it will be essential procedure during technical or dress rehearsals and performances.

D. PROMPTING. There is no hard and fast rule governing when to and when not to prompt. Usually prompting will not start during the first week of rehearsal. During that week both the stage manager and the actor will be occupied marking stage business in their scripts. After business is set and lines learned, prompting starts.

Prompting should be the responsibility of one and the same stage manager throughout rehearsals and opening performances. The actors will become accustomed to the prompter's position, his face, and his voice. The stage manager will discover the actor's memorizing habits, his pauses, his character development, and particular passages in his dialogue he is having difficulty remembering. This rapport between actor and prompter will more often be the clue to when to prompt than any other one thing. It also will be the clue to when *not* to prompt, which is just as important.

Actors' memory patterns or habits vary but generally require one of two types of dialogue promptings. The first is the "key word" or "action word" or "meaning" prompt. The second is the "complete phrase" or "first word" type. These may be illustrated with the following line: "In due time surrender may be expected." Using the first type, the prompter would say, "Surrender." Using the second, "In due time surrender . . ." However, in this line, "Surrender may be expected in due time," the word "surrender" should serve both types. The stage manager must be alert to the individual actor's idiosyncrasies.

When prompting first starts, the prompter should use a clear, strong, normal voice. The actor wants help, not subtleties. As rehearsals progress, the volume may be decreased until the prompter can be heard only on the stage. Whispered prompts are not good. They often can be heard in all parts of the auditorium, whereas a low-volume, normal tone will not. During the final rehearsals the prompter tries to sustain the emotional content of the scene when prompting. This may sound rather fanciful, but it is not. A strident prompt can destroy the mood of a quiet scene, and a drawled prompt can ruin a quick tempo.

Some directors insist that the prompter stop the actor and correct him when he makes a mistake, no matter how small. Certain actors dislike this method. Other directors want prompting done only when the actor has "dried up" completely, and will reserve corrections until the end of the scene. There are those actors who dislike this method. It is a director's problem to decide which type of prompting the individual actor will receive. The stage manager should have this problem settled early in the rehearsal schedule, so that rehearsals will be smooth-running. If corrections are withheld until the end of the scene, the stage manager must record errors for future reference. One method of recording errors is to make light pencil check marks in the manuscript margin and underline the error in the dialogue. These marks can be erased easily after the error is corrected. Often the error is a recurrent one, and then the marks may be left in the script as a signpost that there may be "prompting ahead."

Most stage managers use this technique while "following the script." They watch the actor most of the time, making quick glances at the script to keep succeeding dialogue clearly in mind.

A pencil may be used by placing its point on the line *following* the line being delivered by the actor. When glancing at the script the prompter's eye immediately goes to the correct place in the manuscript, he freshens his mind with succeeding dialogue, advances his pencil another line, and then glances back at the actor. Thus he is always "ahead" of the actor.

Some prompters glue their eyes to the manuscript and prompt by ear only. This has disadvantages. During rehearsals the actor is experimenting. If he interrupts his dialogue, he may be testing the length of a pause for emotional or action reasons. Should the prompter not be watching, he will not realize that the actor is in full control, but will guess that he is "up" and consequently may throw an unwanted and highly disconcerting prompt. Moreover, the only way the stage manager can be in rapport with the actor, can find out what he does at all times, is by looking at him!

Except for the learning period of rehearsals, prompting should be considered an emergency measure, and actors should not use the prompter as a crutch to bolster indifferent memories. However, when a prompt is needed it must be given quickly and clearly. The mental block that creates the need for a prompt must be penetrated. Whatever the cause of the lapse of memory may be, the actor must be set back on the right track before panic sets in.

In the final analysis the best answer to prompting is to insist that the actor learn his dialogue quickly and accurately!

E. ACTING AS ASSISTANT DIRECTOR. The stage manager does not train or direct the actors without explicit permission from the director. Any attempt on his part to do so will be considered an encroachment on the director's province and will not be tolerated. Directing chores turned over to the stage manager will be specific. Such things as blocking out the movements of a crowd of extras and assigning individual lines to members of the crowd fall into this category. If an actor approaches the stage manager with problems of interpretation and characterization, he must be referred to the director.

There are some aspects that come under the general heading of direction that the stage manager does and will be expected to handle. These concern themselves with technical details of the production. If, during the rehearsal, the actor is pantomiming the opening of a window and indicates he thinks it is a sash-type window, when in reality it is a casement window, the stage manager should correct this error. It is not necessary to stop rehearsals to do this, if the mistake concerns this actor only. It may be corrected before or after rehearsal or during a rest period. However, if the error concerns later business, plotting, or dialogue, the attention of the director should be called to the error. These errors should be spotted early in the rehearsal period and corrected immediately. If the actor is permitted to continue in error, he will establish habits that will be upsetting when he finds himself in the scenery.

Unanticipated occasions arise when the director may be late to a rehearsal. The stage manager should take over the running of the rehearsal and prevent loss of rehearsal time. If the director has not made provisions for such emergency absences, the stage manager must use his own judgment. Reviewing work done at previous rehearsals is the general practice. Line rehearsals or walking rehearsals of scenes that have been broken in previously will help the actor set his part. Introducing new material or going on to scenes as yet unrehearsed should not be considered. That is the director's job. Any activity—arranging appointments, discussion of technical matters, checking manuscripts, and so on—that eliminates wasting valuable time should be taken up on these occasions.

In the case of a director who is not a good planner, the stage manager will find himself becoming more and more the assistant director. When and how he assists will depend on many things, but usually such matters as what to rehearse the next day, when to rehearse, time of appointments, and such "technical" functions will fall into the category of duties the stage manager may assume. The stage manager will avoid such things as actor's characterizations, line readings, and other "creative" parts of the director's job unless his assistance is specifically requested. Good common sense and plenty of tact should see a stage manager through rehearsals conducted in this manner.

There are directors who, although quite capable of doing their own planning, will expect the stage manager to prepare rehearsal schedules and such matters for them. The stage manager will be alert to what the director may require from him.

THE NOON (OR MEAL) RECESS

Check:

1. Do all personnel know the time and place to reconvene? This may be a place other than the location of the morning rehearsal.
2. Phone office to advise that morning rehearsal is over and where and when reconvening.
3. Advise director of status of actors on probation.
4. Hold Information Exchange. (See page 32.) This is not an ideal time as the recess is usually only one hour, but some days it is the only available time.

BEFORE DISMISSAL OF ACTORS AT END OF REHEARSAL DAY

Check:

1. Status of actors on probation.
2. Does everyone know the time and place of the next rehearsal? This may mean holding the actors until a conference between the director, star, and stage manager is held.
3. Can any appointments be given out?
4. Have all actors received changes in dialogue?
5. Contact office for late advices for actors.
6. Has Equity Deputy been elected?
7. Have there been any changes of address?
8. Remind actors to take home their scripts and study them.

9. Pick up publicity blanks, tax blanks, etc.
10. Try to gather in some of the pencils that have been borrowed!

AFTER REHEARSAL

I. Staff Conference. Some producers have a staff conference after the day's rehearsing is over. The stage manager attends this conference and delegates the following duties to his assistants:

1. Supervise transfer of ground cloth, rehearsal props, etc. to the new rehearsal hall; or, if no change is being made, see that they are safely stored. See that no personal or company property is left behind.
2. Hold Information Exchange with designers or their assistants.

At the conference the stage manager will help arrange appointments and future schedules and will take notes pertinent to his department. He will pass on these notes to his assistants later.

II. Stage Managers' Daily Meeting. If the producer does not have regular and formal staff meetings, the stage manager's first duty is to check with the office for advices. The producer may not have been able to attend rehearsals and will want a progress report. This is the time to discuss with the producer or business manager all problems that have arisen during the day that the stage manager cannot settle.

When immediate matters (staff conference, disposal of ground cloth, etc.) are settled, the stage manager and his assistants will gather together for their daily meeting, or Clearing House. The purpose of this meeting is to tie in all the loose ends in the day's business, to exchange ideas, and to plan future activity.

This stage managers' meeting often is held in the producer's office, where stationery, typewriters, and other office facilities, especially telephones, are available. If the office has a PBX switchboard, a half-hour's instruction in its operation from the office switchboard operator will be invaluable to the stage manager, since this meeting normally is held after regular office hours. The business manager will make arrangements for these meetings, furnishing keys to the office and advising the office building employees that the stage managers are bona fide members of his staff and may be admitted to the building at irregular hours. At this meeting the following should be accomplished:

A. ROUTINE

1. Discuss notes taken at staff conference.
2. Make a list of the following day's appointments in triplicate, one for the producer, director, and stage managers, and arrange transportation if necessary. Separate appointment slips should be made for each actor, showing type of appointment, date and time, address, best means of transportation.
3. Bring actors file up-to-date.
4. Clear up status of actors in abeyance.
5. Bring expense account up-to-date.
6. Bring address list up-to-date.
7. Hold Information Exchange with designer (if not already held).
8. Bring prompt script up-to-date. Where applicable, notes should be transferred into the technical plots.

   Many of the stage manager's rehearsal notes will be written hastily. Some stage directions may be a series of arrows; actors' stage positions may be shown by a small diagram, e.g., a group around a table. These should be clarified and inserted into the manuscript while they are in mind. It should be remembered that the final manuscript will be reproduced on a standard typewriter.

   In revising the manuscript, page numbers should be retained until all active manuscripts, those used by actors and staff members, can be renumbered simultaneously. Completely renumbering the prompt script pages daily is an unnecessary chore and makes reference between manuscripts held by different staff members difficult. Added

pages can bear the preceding page number plus an identifying "*a*," "*b*," "*c*," etc.

If the production secretary is hired to keep the manuscript freshly typed, his services should be used at this
time. The secretary can relieve the stage manager of much
typing, and the stage manager can furnish the secretary
information about stage directions.

Many stage managers have a practice of not "cleaning
up" the prompt script after a certain point in the rehearsal
period. This practice has sound foundations and will be
discussed later in Part Three, Section Two. However, during these early rehearsals the manuscript must be kept
fresh.

A manuscript is not up-to-date unless a theater-wise person, unfamiliar with the production, can read it and understand it at sight.

B. TRAINING ASSISTANTS. This meeting can be a valuable opportunity for the stage manager to train his assistants. The stage
manager's sights are set on the performance of the play. He has
been planning and revising performance pattern constantly. He
will share his plans with his assistants and accept suggestions
from them. One of the stage manager's most necessary qualities is
an ability to anticipate. Experience, of course, is the greatest help
a stage manager may have in anticipating. Yet anticipation is also
a frame of mind, a point of view, usually a questioning one. This
handbook's primary purpose is to help the inexperienced anticipate his problems. The experienced stage manager will help his
assistants, particularly with problems peculiar to a particular production.

1. *Division of Duties.* Just as rehearsal duties are departmen-
talized, performance duties, too, will be split up among the stage
managers. It is wise to carry over rehearsal duties to the performance. The assistant in charge of checking actors at rehearsal
will be in charge of checking them at performances. The assistant

in charge of rehearsal props should be in charge of performance props.

Most stage managers go through the play line by line, move by move, and plan each stage manager's action, physical and mental. They do this when all assistants are in attendance, as each must be familiar with the other's duties. It will be decided how each cue is accomplished, how each element of the production is checked, and who will supervise the checking—be the double-check. They will study and revise the performance pattern, ironing out difficulties and conflicts. No element is too small or unimportant or obvious not to be considered and discussed. These discussions of the performance pattern should be a free exchange of ideas and suggestions between the stage managers.

2. *Emergencies. a) Anticipation and the Performance Pattern.* The stage manager should develop the habit of thinking out loud when with his assistants, and should encourage them to do the same. Continual asking of the question "What do I do if . . . ?" and then finding the answer, will anticipate most emergencies, and anticipation prevents apprehension. The more completely the stage managers foresee emergencies, and have mental drills of their procedure for emergencies, the less apprehensive they will be about them. The question "What do I do if . . . ?" ceases to be formidable, if the stage managers have trained themselves by correct thinking patterns to act quickly and properly in emergencies.

The reader should not get the impression that the stage manager goes about in a state bordering on panic. He does not, or he should not. Nevertheless, things will go wrong. The best defense against errors is a strong performance pattern.

Many anecdotes are told about backstage accidents or emergencies. An actor fainted or the scenery collapsed, but, because of quick action, the "audience never knew." Most of these stories are true. The credit given individuals for covering the error is well placed. But it will be found that, because of anticipation and thorough training of all departments, the play had a good performance pattern, and that, basically, the pattern was the real hero.

School children have a performance pattern in their fire drills. Soldiers learn a performance pattern in their many drills and maneuvers. These patterns are time-tested over months and years, and so new school children and recruits can be molded to the pattern quickly. The importance of performance pattern in the production of a play must be emphasized, because each play is new and different and not time-tested. Each day of rehearsal, each technical or dress rehearsal, and each tryout performance will see changes and refinements in the pattern until, in only a few days or possibly hours, the final pattern is set. The need for a good pattern is as important in the production of the play as in any other activity, but the limitation of time is more acute in the theater than in most other professions. Obviously any planning, any anticipation of production elements that facilitates the establishing of a good, strong performance pattern must be considered. These stage manager Clearing Houses are an excellent time to accomplish the groundwork for a good performance pattern.

The stage manager not only poses questions and finds answers; he must be attentive to those questions his assistants ask and, particularly, to answers or solutions they may propose. Many a fine technician has learned new methods by watching a duffer blunder through a problem to its solution. The assistants' questions also serve as a double-check to prevent overlooking the obvious.

b) Material Understudies. Many disasters or emergencies caused by breakage or mechanical failure can be avoided by having material or production understudies. Just as the actor has his understudy, the properties, lights, sound, etc. must have their understudies or alternates. Obviously a complete alternate production cannot be standing by, but any material thing, the loss or mechanical failure of which would upset the plot or smooth action of the play, must have an alternate. This is especially true of perishable, fragile, or intricate mechanical things. Such items as phone bells, cigarettes and matches, glassware, special spotlights, phonograph records, and flashlights are obvious examples. The most famous example is the cover gun held offstage, ready to fire in case the actor's gun misfires. These material understudies will be spotted when the stage managers are asking each other, "What do I do if . . . ?" Arrangements should be made to have them prepared or manufactured by the appropriate production department.

FINAL DAILY CHECK LIST

1. Time and place of next rehearsal
2. Time and place of appointments
3. Status of actors on probation
4. Changes of address
5. Status of understudies
6. Has Clearing House been held?
7. Is the prompt script up-to-date?

REHEARSAL PROPERTIES

Only substitute rehearsal properties may be used during rehearsals, unless a property man has been hired. This is an IA (International Alliance of Theatrical Stage Employees and Motion Picture Operators of the United States and Canada—for obvious reasons called the IA or the Stage Hands Union) ruling and should not be violated.

A rehearsal prop is any simple makeshift that simulates the real prop but could not be construed to be the real prop. Paper cups are suitable rehearsal cocktail glasses; glassware of any sort might be construed to be the real thing and should not be used. A rolled newspaper is a suitable rehearsal substitute for a shiny, brass telescope; an old battered, black telescope is too close to the real thing—don't use it.

If a property man has been hired to handle a ground cloth for rehearsals, then he may be used for handling other properties, and all kinds of props, real or substitute, may be used.

In the event that an actor must read from a book, letter, etc. during the performance, the stage manager should receive instructions from the director as to whether or not the dialogue is to be inserted into the book so that the actor may actually read it. These props should be prepared by the stage managers to insure accuracy, and may be used at rehearsals.

READING REHEARSALS

In the foregoing portion on rehearsals it has been assumed that the director will want to start immediately with the actors "on their feet," with "walking rehearsals." However, many directors prefer to spend from one day to a week or more "reading the play." These readings are usually conducted by the director and are periods of intense concentration for discussion of characterizations, motivations, and reading of lines. The stage manager will see that quiet is maintained and interruptions avoided.

Following the readings the actors will get on their feet, and rehearsals will proceed as described before. The actor will be advanced considerably in learning lines and characterization.

SPECIAL REHEARSALS

The stage manager will arrange with the director for special rehearsals and performances for sound recordings. As recording is expensive, these rehearsals should be held before the time set aside for actual recording and not in the recording studio.

Other special rehearsals include fencing lessons, music lessons, and the like, and should be plotted with the director.

PART THREE

Rehearsals, Final Weeks

The final weeks of rehearsal see the ·beginning of the assembling of the production and concrete preparations for the setup, technical and dress rehearsals, and the tryout tour. All elements of a production interlock, but, for purposes of analysis and study, they are kept separate through the first two sections of this Part of the handbook. The third section brings all elements together. And so the reader should bear in mind that Section One (the technical side of the production) and Section Two (the acting side) are parallel movements, interlocking at many points and moving together toward Section Three (the technical and dress rehearsals), where they are joined together for a performance.

The high point of these weeks, before the technical and dress rehearsals, is the actor run-throughs of the play. And so it is common to find all departments thinking of these weeks as the "run-through period." This handbook uses the term "run-through period" in that all-inclusive sense.

SECTION ONE—TECHNICAL ELEMENTS

POLISHING THE ELEMENTS

I. Checking "Specials." Before the run-through period the director will have checked and approved all "specials." This will include everything of an unusual nature, e.g., all sound effects including recordings, all unusual costumes, peculiar properties, and, if possible, special lighting effects. Extra rehearsals may be held for these "specials" before or during the run-throughs, while there is still time to make substantial changes.

II. Technical Check List. The run-through period is a time when the stage manager should make a final check list of technical questions he must answer but cannot until the scenery is set up. This list includes such things as exact location of offstage objects referred to by the actors, limitations on the actors' movements imposed by the structure of the theater, peculiar sight lines, difficulties during scene shifts, and such problems.

III. Technical Plots. The stage manager will have been elaborating his technical plots as well as other portions of his prompt script and will see that copies of the plots are in the hands of the department heads. By this time the business manager will have hired the production stage crew and decided when it starts work. If there is to be an out-of-town tryout, this crew must include a carpenter, property man, electrician, and a wardrobe mistress. Where there are sound effects utilizing electronic equipment, a sound operator is added. Large productions may include one or more assistants in each department. Productions that do not make an out-of-town tryout tour may not have production crew hands in all departments, but may utilize the house crew heads in their stead.

The property man receives notice of all additions and changes to the property plot. Before the setup this plot will be brought into as near a final edition as possible and discussed in detail with the property man. There will be certain items of decoration known only to the designer, and these will not be included; but no property concerned with the action or plot of the play may be omitted. This property plot will be an elaboration of the plot indicated in Part One and consists of three sections for each scene or act: set props, onstage small or hand props, and offstage props, with brief notes on placement and preparation. The actor using the hand prop should be indicated, but only identifying descriptions need be given in this working plot. Clarity and easy reference are essential.

Cue sheets for each scene and act should be given to the electrician and the sound man. These cue sheets do not concern themselves with the mechanics of accomplishing the cue but list the nature of the cues in order of occurrence. Using the revised master cue sheet, the stage manager separates each department's cues into separate cue sheets.

LIGHTING CUE SHEET

ACT ONE, Scene 1		
Cue number	Cue	Description
1	Hand signal from Stg. Mgr.	Table light desk R – ON
2	Hand signal	Table light desk R – OFF
3	Gunshot	All lights – FLICKER
4	Hand signal	Outside window – SLOW FADE TO OUT by end of scene (6 min.)
5	ACT CURTAIN (end of scene)	Front Lights DIM OUT with lowering curtain
ACT ONE, Scene 2		
6	ACT CURTAIN (opening of scene)	Front Lights DIM UP TO MARK with rising curtain
7	Hand signal	Hall light U.C. – OFF
8	etc.	etc.

The sound cue sheet is composed in the same manner as the lighting cue sheet.

The designer will furnish the wardrobe mistress with a costume plot, but the stage manager should be prepared to supplement it if necessary. Understudies' costumes must be remembered.

The stage manager now enters the master cue sheet into the

prompt script. This is done by separating the cues, or groups of cues, and entering them into the script on the pages where they occur. (See Appendix B.) In this way the stage manager has all the cues, dialogue and technical, before him, running concurrently on the same pages. He rarely works with a separate cue sheet, as this requires shifting his attention back and forth between the dialogue in the prompt script and cues on the cue sheet.

PREPARATION FOR THE SETUP AND TRYOUT TOUR

This section should be read in conjunction with Part Five, "Touring," as they supplement each other.

I. Itinerary. A complete itinerary of the tryout tour should be made and a copy furnished everyone in the production. This itinerary will include:

Dates of:

Actor's trunk pickup

Scenery pickup

Train departure and arrival time (station and R.R.) for crew

Train departure and arrival time (station and R.R.) for acting company

Rehearsal schedule, including type and kind

Performance dates and times, matinees and eves

Photographing the production

II. Setup Schedule. The members of the staff will decide on a setup schedule which will be very detailed. It might be as follows:

Mon., Oct. 10— 8:00 A.M.—Call at baggage cars

8:30   —Call at theater and load in—start hanging and assembling

12:00   —Lunch

1:00 P.M.—Hanging and assembling

5:30   —Dinner

7:00   —Hanging and assembling—continue until only odds and ends left

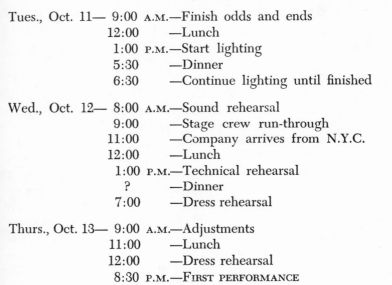

Tues., Oct. 11— 9:00 A.M.—Finish odds and ends
     12:00 —Lunch
     1:00 P.M.—Start lighting
     5:30 —Dinner
     6:30 —Continue lighting until finished

Wed., Oct. 12— 8:00 A.M.—Sound rehearsal
     9:00 —Stage crew run-through
     11:00 —Company arrives from N.Y.C.
     12:00 —Lunch
     1:00 P.M.—Technical rehearsal
     ? —Dinner
     7:00 —Dress rehearsal

Thurs., Oct. 13— 9:00 A.M.—Adjustments
     11:00 —Lunch
     12:00 —Dress rehearsal
     8:30 P.M.—FIRST PERFORMANCE

III. Number of Stage Hands. The number of stage hands needed for the setup will be discussed by the staff members, and a call for them will be placed with the union local at the place of the setup. A discussion of the number of stage hands needed for dress rehearsals and performances will be found in Section Three of this Part of the handbook.

IV. O.P. (Opposite Prompt) Side. A considerable time before leaving for the tryout tour, the stage manager will plot the problems he will face if the prompt side of the stage in the tryout theaters is opposite to the one in the New York theater the production will occupy, and opposite to the side he has been using in rehearsal and has been visualizing in preparations for the New York performance. Having anticipated such a change, it should present no difficulty when met.

The prompt side of the stage is determined by the facilities offered by the theater, the placement of the fixed equipment. Generally, the prompt side is the same as the location of the house switchboard and company switch. Other equipment normally found on the prompt side are the house curtain control and the pin rail. The company switch is the source of power for the production switchboards, and they are placed adjacent to it. Consequently, to be nearby for cuing purposes, the prompt desk will be on the same side as the production switchboards. Exceptions and variations are encountered, but the above system for determining the prompt side is standard.

V. Advice Sheet. The advance agent prepares an "advice sheet," which he delivers to the theater managers in the cities to be played. Most of this sheet consists of information pertinent to the advance agent's own department—program copy, marquee arrangements, posters, and publicity interviews—but it also contains information for the technical departments of the out-of-town theaters. The production crew heads will furnish this information to the advance agent, but the stage manager keeps himself informed of the contents of the technical part of the advice sheet, and has it on his list of Things Not To Be Forgotten. Such things as hanging plots, dimensions and positions of traps to be cut in the stage floor, special electrical current, and so on are examples. By sending these advices ahead, work may be done by the local stage hands before the production arrives, and valuable setup time is saved. The advance agent also makes preparations for the acting company, such as permits for child actors and arranging a call for extras.

VI. Fireproofing. Scenery, draperies, and other properties obtained through reputable theatrical supply houses are automatically fireproofed (more properly, the term is flameproofed). This is in the business manager's province, but is on the stage manager's list of Things Not To Be Forgotten.

During the setup in each city played, an inspector from the local fire department will examine all inflammable articles and will test them with an open flame, often a lighted match but sometimes a red-hot blowtorch. An article that does not pass inspection must be flameproofed before a performance may be given. While on tour, the stage manager will see that the firm or individual doing the flameproofing furnishes a dated and signed certificate or affidavit describing the articles treated and affirming that the treatment has been accomplished.

Open flames on the stage must be circumvented by some means. The fire departments in most cities will not permit them. Electric substitutes for candles, oil lamps, and fires in fireplaces have been in use for so long that audiences accept them as conventional stage effects.

Onstage ashtrays should contain a film of water so that lighted cigarettes will not smolder. Exits should be equipped with water or sand buckets in which lighted cigarettes may be doused when carried offstage by actors.

Fire inspectors are serious-minded, responsible individuals. Evidence of fire-prevention equipment and precautions will gain the inspector's respect and co-operation. Carelessness or disregard of precautions may lead to severe penalties.

THE SETUP—PREPARATION FOR THE TECHNICAL AND DRESS REHEARSALS

The stage manager will turn over the running of the actor rehearsals to his assistants and will spend most of his time in the theater where the setup is being made. In the case of an out-of-town tryout tour, the original setup is usually made in the theater of the first stand. The stage manager will travel with the technical staff, preceding the acting company by one or several days. In this handbook it is presumed a tryout tour is being made.

I. Work Schedule. Plan a work schedule with the production crew heads and the company manager and keep a time sheet of the crew's working hours. Insist on proper rest periods and meal hours.

II. House Doctor. Determine how to locate and obtain the services of the house physician quickly.

III. Additional Rehearsal Space. If the first tryout stand is relatively close to New York City, the acting company will remain in New York while the setup is being made and will time its arrival at the tryout stand to coincide with the completion of the setup. Then technical and dress rehearsals will start immediately. However at future stands, or if the acting company accompanies the scenery and technical staff, rehearsal space other than the stage of the theater must be provided, because the stage will be utilized for setup purposes. Theater lobbies and smoking rooms are used if available and large enough. Ballrooms and dining rooms in near-by hotels are alternate choices, as are empty theaters, if the tryout city should have them. Fraternal organizations have meeting halls they sometimes rent for such purposes. The local theater manager will have suggestions. As these extra rehearsal spaces are often rented, the problem should be discussed with the company manager before the stage manager leaves New York, since the company manager will pay the bill.

IV. Assigning Dressing Rooms.   It should be remembered that dressing rooms are assigned with the best interests of the production in mind. Prestige, prejudice, or whim are secondary. If there are contractual agreements between the actor and management concerning dressing rooms to be provided, the business manager will advise the stage manager of such agreements. Normally the assignment of dressing rooms solves itself easily.

Keeping in mind the following factors for each actor, the stage manager should have no difficulty: The proximity of the dressing room to the stage, or the side of the stage on which it is located, is important to actors with many costume changes, or with a quick change not made onstage. Age and sex of the actor; location of toilets, showers, and washrooms; size, ventilation, and anterooms; and condition of the dressing room itself are all factors to be considered. Generally speaking, if there are two actors of equal importance to the production, and one is a woman, she will have the better dressing room.

If there is no wardrobe room, a dressing room should be assigned the wardrobe mistress as a workroom.

A list of dressing room assignments should be posted on the

call board. Copies should be given the wardrobe mistress to expedite distribution of costumes and to the production property man for a guide in distributing the actors' theater trunks.

The dressing rooms should be checked for cleanliness, lights, mirrors, chairs, hangers, toilet facilities, and keys to lock doors. Changes needed in chairs and carpets should be reported to the house property man, lighting changes to the house electrician, and faulty locks to the house carpenter.

V. Prompt Desk. Place the prompt desk, allowing sufficient room for prompting and cuing. Locate and test all cuing devices.

VI. Supervision of Departments. The stage manager must be available at all times during the setup. In general he works through his production chiefs when giving suggestions or corrections to individual stage hands. This is common sense delegation of authority and responsibility, but in the heat of activity it may be neglected. It should not be. Much of the stage manager's time will be spent answering questions from members of the different departments. Some typical problems the stage manager may face, and a list of personnel involved, follow:

A. Carpentry Department. Placing portable dressing rooms, practicality of scenery, sight lines, masking, cross-overs, safety, etc.

The production carpenter is known as "the carpenter," and his assistant is often the flyman. Members of the Carpentry Department are under the house carpenter and are called "grips."

B. Property Departments. Arrangement of props onstage, placement of small props, preparation of edibles, identification of props, etc.

Production property man is "the property man." House property man has charge of the "clearers" or "handlers."

C. Electrical Department. Positions of onstage fixtures, switches, etc. Location of special spots. Number and position of work lights.

Production electrician is "the electrician." The house electrician has charge of the "operators."

D. WARDROBE DEPARTMENT.   Identification of costumes and accessories.

Sometimes the wardrobe mistress needs assistance in preparing costumes and hires members of the local union. They are often called "wardrobe women" (or men), and, if they assist actors to change their costumes, they are called "dressers." These are separate from the actors' personal servants, who are usually known as "maids" or "valets."

Make arrangements to protect the actors' costumes from damage or dirt backstage. The backstage area is often dirty, especially during technical and dress rehearsals. The best solution is to get the area cleaned, but the pressure of time may not allow this. Also floors, narrow passageways, and cross-overs can never be made spotless. The use of cloths on the floor and on walls and particularly around stage machinery will help protect costumes. Duplicate sets of cloths should be available, so that replacements are on hand when one set is being laundered.

E. SOUND DEPARTMENT.   Locate equipment, test effects, get volumes, and establish cuing procedure.

F. GENERAL.   Try to get the answers for technical check list prepared during run-throughs (see page 60).

VII. Lighting.   Watch the lighting of the show and assist. During the lighting the stage manager assists the designer (or lighting specialist) by walking through the positions the actors assume during the business of the play. He checks special effects, checks placement of onstage fixtures such as table lamps and wall switches, times light changes such as dims, and relays information between the designer in the auditorium and the electrician backstage.

During the lighting the stage manager will take copious notes, which must furnish:

A. *Specifications for Each Instrument*
    1. Identity number and type of each
    2. Exact position when mounted
    3. Focus

4. Color
5. Area covered by light
6. Any special notes

B. *Cue Sheet*
1. Instruments used in each scene
2. Intensity of each instrument
3. Instruments involved in any cue or change

Other terms for these two sets of notes are, (A) "hanging plot," and (B) "switchboard setup or hookup."

The stage manager must be able to reproduce the designer's lighting quickly and accurately.

VIII. Orchestras. If an orchestra is used in the pit or backstage, arrange for its accommodation.

The management may not plan to use a pit orchestra in New York and may not wish one on the road, but very often theaters in tryout cities have contracts with the local musicians, who will play willy-nilly! Sometimes the management will welcome a pit orchestra. In any event the music to be played should be decided. This falls to the stage manager sometimes. He should arrange a meeting with the orchestra leader, at which time the music to be used, the length of the overture and intermission music, and methods of cuing can be decided.

IX. Stage Crew Run-through. Before the full technical or dress rehearsals which include actors, a run-through for the stage crews should be held. The complexity of the production will decide whether or not this should be done by all crews simultaneously or by each department singly. During this run-through, all shifts of scenery, sound cues, lighting changes and cues, placement and disposal of properties, and curtain cues must be accomplished. All mechanical adjustments may be made without the distraction that a company of actors brings. It should be remembered that the stage crew in a very few days must adjust itself to a new play that the playwright, producer, director, designers, and actors have taken months to devise. The stage manager must help make this adjustment painless.

The stage manager will be most helpful to the production stage crew if he acts as a general overseer rather than concentrates on one particular department. He can assign his assistants as overseers of individual parts of the scene change. During scene shifts his traditional observation post is Downstage Center, facing Upstage with his back against the house curtain. In this position he is out of the way and can observe all departments simultaneously and can gather material to help co-ordinate the change.

The stage manager must plan where the actor is to wait during the changes, where to go after an exit, and where to wait for entrance cues. If he is alert to the idiosyncrasies of the technical end of the production, he is better equipped to watch over the welfare and safety of all backstage personnel.

X. Performance Check List.   The stage manager does not have time to check every item involved in a quick change of scenery. He makes a special "performance check list" for use during the performance, especially just before ringing up the curtain on a scene. This list is small and includes just those things that vitally concern the plot or business during the ensuing scene. These things are most often properties, but will include lighting equipment, costumes, and the scenery. If these items are prepared and in place, the performance may proceed; without them there is no performance. E.g., the revolver in the desk drawer, with which the hero shoots the villain, *must be in place and prepared* or the show goes out the window; the antimacassar on the chair is decorative and indicative of character, but its absence in no way interrupts the plot or action. The revolver is on the list, the antimacassar is not. Again, the door D.R. *must be open* so that the hero can see the villain's approach; the door U.L. to a closet may be open or shut, and it will not concern the play vitally. The door D.R. is on the list, the door U.L. is not. This list should be kept as small as possible. Its contents are much the same as the "material understudies" mentioned on page 55 but are not necessarily identical.

XI. Personnel Watching Setup.   Actors and other production members should not be discouraged from watching the setup. The desire to watch the progress of "their" production is a healthy sign and should be encouraged. However, make sure that all watchers keep out from under foot and do their watching from a safe place. The stage manager is responsible for the safety of all persons backstage. Accidents are rare, and the producer carries insurance to protect personnel *who have a legitimate reason* for being backstage. This does not include wives, sweethearts, or the doorman's Great-aunt Sue. Should an unauthorized person be involved in an accident, the stage manager is in an awkward situation.

SECTION TWO—ACTING ELEMENTS
POLISHING THE ELEMENTS

I. Program Copy.   The publicity agent is responsible for the composition of the program, but the aid of the stage manager is usually enlisted to check correctness of names of characters, names of actors, production credits, and such material.

II. The Prompt Script.   Mention was made previously (page 53) that some time during rehearsals the stage manager stops "cleaning up" his prompt script. That time is now—when run-throughs start. By this time major dialogue or stage business changes have been made, and all future alterations should be small. If the stage manager has a "clean" script at the start of the run-throughs, the script should not need another retyping until after opening night.

This is not a hard and fast rule and there are exceptions, but the stage managers who follow this plan do so for the following reason. Within a few days after the run-throughs start, the stage manager will be away from rehearsals, concentrating on the setup. He will return to his prompt script only for technical and dress rehearsals. He will not have time to transfer his cues into a fresh manuscript or to familiarize himself with new page sequences. When he returns to his prompt script, he will want it to fit like an old shoe. A new script could easily throw him out of the pattern he has been establishing. Obviously, if further major changes are made, a fresh typing of the section concerned may be necessary.

III. Understudy Progress.   During all rehearsal periods the stage manager must not lose sight of the progress understudies are making. Check them constantly to see that they are keeping their dialogue and stage business up-to-date, that they are attending all rehearsals, that provisions have been made for their costuming, that they have learned their lines. Rehearse them when possible.

IV. Inspecting the Scenery.   Some scenic studios have facilities for setting up the scenery in their shops, and they do so as a sort of preliminary setup and as a check against possible construction errors. Arrangements should be made for the actors to visit the studio and inspect the scenery while it is assembled, even though it may be unpainted. If possible this visit should be made before the run-throughs because added and concrete knowledge of the scenery will make the run-through considerably more real.

V. The Run-through.   During the last stages of rehearsal, the director will have complete run-throughs of the play. The purpose of a run-through is to consolidate the direction, establish tempo to the play as a whole, create a feeling of unity in the acting company, and get the playing time. This is a part of the period when the director is "polishing" the play.

The run-through gives the stage managers an opportunity to test and adjust the performance pattern they have planned and discussed during their Clearing Houses. It also offers them a chance to give the actors a preview of their cuing procedure.

The stage manager should try to approximate a performance atmosphere as completely as is possible without scenery, costumes, lighting, and properties. He will see that the actors receive proper warning calls; that all sound, light, and other cues are given and that the effect is achieved or indicated; that an accurate record of the playing time is kept; and that a maximum number of substitute rehearsal props are available and used. Although the director is occupied primarily with acting during the run-through, it is desirable to incorporate into it as many of the special effects, costumes, and properties as are legal and practicable. An actor should have as many opportunities to become familiar with these mechanics as is feasible.

An example of a "special" that may be incorporated into the run-through or earlier rehearsal is the use of pieces of cloth which actresses may pin to their street dresses to simulate trains. The costumer will furnish these trains, but the stage manager will take charge of them as he does substitute rehearsal properties.

A chart, on one sheet of paper, should be prepared, on which the running time of each run-through and all technical and dress rehearsals may be entered. This chart is useful for comparison purposes and is referred to frequently by all staff members.

PREPARATION FOR THE TRYOUT TOUR

I. Itinerary. The itinerary described on page 62 will be furnished all members of the acting company. The stage managers will be sure that members of the company inexperienced in touring understand all parts of the itinerary.

II. Hotel Reservations. At least two weeks before leaving New York for the out-of-town tryout the advance agent will furnish the stage manager with a list of hotels in the cities to be played. This list will include the names of hotels, types of accommodations, rates, and distance from the theater. The stage manager will make these lists available to the actors and will press them to make reservations immediately. Most actors prefer to make their own reservations, but, if they are unable to obtain them, it is the management's responsibility to get them for the actor. This is an Actors' Equity ruling and was designed primarily to assist the touring actor when sudden shifts of schedule, or routing into crowded cities, are made by the management. If the actor relies on the management to get his hotel reservations, he must accept any reasonable accommodation offered, or pay for its cancellation if the hotel so demands. It is understood that inability on the actor's part to get a reservation means that the actor cannot get *any* suitable accommodation, not that he cannot get the exact room, at the exact price, in the exact hotel he chooses. Thus it behooves the stage manager to keep after the actor and see that reservations are made early. Moreover, as trunks are carried in the scenery baggage cars, they will arrive at the tryout city one to several days before the actor, and the local transfer company must know where to deliver the trunks. Storage, at the actor's expense, is sometimes charged on unde-livered trunks. Generally, managements are extremely co-opera-tive in helping the actor get the hotel accommodation he desires. Nevertheless, making hotel reservations early is always good practice.

III. Trunks. An Actors' Equity rule puts on the actor the responsibility of transporting his personal trunk to the railroad station in New York City, but the manager must reimburse the actor for the cost of such transportation up to three dollars. How-ever, as the manager usually does not want the trunk at a rail-road station (baggage cars are loaded in areas away from sta-tions), the following has become the accepted and expected standard procedure for handling actors' personal trunks.

It is the stage manager's responsibility to see that a pickup list of actors' trunks is furnished to the property man. The prop-erty man arranges with the transfer men to do the actual col-lecting of the trunks. This collection and delivery of trunks is an obligation of the management, but there are certain limitations the actor should understand. The transfer companies limit their pickup area to central Manhattan and have specifications the actor must meet. The instruction given the actor to have his trunk "ready and downstairs by nine o'clock" means just that. Transfer companies are not required to wait for last-minute packing, or to go above or below street level, to make a collection. Should the actor not meet the specifications for preparing his trunk for collection, and the trunk is left behind, it will be his responsibility to transport his trunk to the next city at his own expense.

If the actor lives outside the collection area, the management furnishes funds to enable the actor to have his trunk transported into the collection area. E.g., an actor living in Westchester may have his trunk checked into Grand Central Terminal at the management's expense (provided the cost is not more than three dollars), and then have the transfer people pick up the trunk from the Terminal. In this case the actor will turn over his claim check to the stage manager, who will attach it to the trunk pickup list furnished the property man. It is advisable for the stage manager to keep a separate record of the claim check in case of loss.

All personnel in the production, who use a trunk while touring, receive the same consideration as the actor, and their names are included on all trunk lists.

Before the property man leaves for the next city, he should be furnished with a trunk delivery list, which he turns over to the transfer men at the next stand. This list has two parts—hotel trunks and theater trunks. All hotel trunks are listed separately under the actors' names, and the hotels to which they are to be delivered are indicated. Depending on the length of the tryout tour, practically all personnel may need a hotel trunk.

Today the wardrobe mistress carries all women's costumes and make-up and most men's costumes and make-up; so no actress should need a theater trunk, and only those actors who furnish their own costumes will require one. Wardrobe Department trunks, or trunks used for transporting draperies, properties, and other production elements, are *not* theater trunks. This is an important distinction. When moving a production, most transfer companies charge a flat rate by the "load," plus a more expensive rate for "pieces." Actors' trunks, both hotel and theater, are considered pieces, and are charged for accordingly. Wardrobe Department trunks, drapery trunks, etc. are part of the production and receive the load rate. Putting them on a theater-trunk list would shift them to the piece rate, a needless expense.

A new pickup list should be made by the stage manager for each city. This may be identical with the delivery list used on arrival, but often it is not. Actors have been known to shift hotels several times in the course of a week. The expense of shifting a trunk from hotel to hotel is borne by the actor. The management pays for *one* delivery and *one* pickup at each stand.

The management furnishes printed trunk labels showing the name of the play and whether it is a hotel or theater trunk. The actor should affix the proper one to his trunk. The publicity agent has these labels printed. He gives them to the stage manager, who distributes them to the actors and turns over the remaining supply to the property man.

IV. The Call. Several days before a company is to be transported to another city the company manager will post "the Call" or the call sheet. This is a standardized, printed form on which information is inserted pertaining to all personnel. This information includes:

Name of next stand (city)

Name of the theater

Number of matinee and evening performances to be played, their dates and times, and matinee days

Time of train departure and arrival, R.R. station, for actors

Time of train departure and arrival, R.R. station, for crews

Date and time of hotel-trunk pickup

Date, time, place baggage cars spotted at next stand

Date, time of call at baggage cars for unloading

Date, time of call at theater to load in scenery

Name and phone number of next stand's transfer company

Time of orchestra rehearsal

Hotel list for next stand (Separate lists of hotels for several stands are usually furnished days or weeks in advance of posting the Call.)

Any special notes, such as time of call to interview extras

Once posted on the bulletin board (call board), the Call may *not be removed by anyone* except the head production stage carpenter and/or the stage manager and company manager. The latter will remove it only to make changes. No one else, not even the producer, will remove the call from the call board, even temporarily, for any reason.

After the final performance and after the production has been removed from the theater to the baggage cars, the head production carpenter is the last member of the company to leave the theater. He is also the first to arrive at the new theater, and so he will remove the Call and carry it with him for reference purposes. Sometimes, if the crew travels ahead of the acting company and the stage manager accompanies the crew, the carpenter will request that the stage manager carry the Call for safekeeping. The stage manager will defer to the carpenter's wishes.

When leaving New York for its first tryout stand, the company will have been advised of the information on the Call days and weeks in advance of the actual posting of the Call. In this case its posting is something of an added formality. However, all future Calls at all future stands will be of vital interest to all personnel. The stage manager must see that inexperienced personnel familiarize themselves with it. It is the individual's responsibility, thereafter, to keep current with information pertinent to himself.

V. Personnel Check-off List. The stage manager and his assistants should have a "personnel check-off list." This list will include all personnel making the tryout tour and can be combined with the out-of-town address list. Such a list is useful for checking off the arrival of personnel at trains, meetings, rehearsals, etc.

VI. Children and Animals. The use of children or animals in a production must be approved by local city departments and societies. Arrangements for approval are made by the general manager in New York City and by the advance agent on the road; but this, too, is one of the things the stage manager must have on his list of Things Not To Be Forgotten. In general, the various Gerry societies that handle this matter are very co-opera-tive, but arrangements take time. The child's background, home life, health, family finances, and schooling must be investigated; the animal's health, transportation, quartering, and feeding must be approved. Any last-minute attempt to rush through a permit will be looked upon with suspicion by the authorities.

SECTION THREE—ASSEMBLING ALL ELEMENTS

At this point all the technical elements and all the acting ele-ments meet and are fused together.

MANAGING THE TECHNICAL AND DRESS REHEARSALS

Technical rehearsals differ from the stage crew run-through in that they include actors. The technical rehearsal aims to co-ordi-nate the technical and acting departments of a production, and time is taken to correct errors. Sometimes whole scenes are re-peated. Dress rehearsals, on the other hand, are really perform-ances, and an attempt is made to progress through the play without stopping, even though the production may falter badly at times.

Technical rehearsals normally include all elements of the pro-duction, but emphasis is on mechanics rather than acting. How-ever, the term is used rather loosely to include special rehearsals of separate departments. These are more properly called "light-ing rehearsals," "sound rehearsals," "costume parades," or, as in this handbook, "stage crew rehearsals" and "run-throughs."

The stage manager will try to run both technical and dress re-hearsals as nearly like performances as possible. As managing the performance is taken up in detail in Part Four, only added sug-gestions are made here.

I. Schedule.   Plan a schedule and stick to it.

II. Taking Charge.   The stage manager is now in charge, and he must assume full control. To be in charge and remain in charge, the stage manager must not be distracted from his post at the prompt desk.

It seems inevitable that at the exact moment the stage manager is forced to abandon his prompt script some actor needs a prompt. This is not necessarily Fate playing a cruel trick. The break in routine, or performance pattern, that has distracted the stage manager may be the same thing that has upset the actor. The stage manager must learn to override these distractions and keep his primary focus onstage.

The greatest distraction, dividing his attention to answer questions, can be reduced if backstage personnel are trained as suggested on page 46.

III. Irregularities. Advise the actors of all technical idiosyncrasies and unforeseen production elements discovered during the setup.

IV. Maintaining Quiet. As personnel will be tired, nerves will be raw, tempers short.

V. Making Corrections. Work as quickly as possible, but take time to correct and adjust. Don't be stampeded. A mistake must be understood to be corrected. When a difficult cue or scene change is approaching, it is advisable to stop the rehearsal, explain the problem to crew and actors, explain the solution to the problem, and then proceed to attempt the solution after everyone understands his part. The stage manager, of course, has analyzed these problems from the day he first read the manuscript, has investigated them during the setup, and will be prepared with the solution. These interruptions to correct or avoid errors will save confusion and time and possibly accidents. Remember, the shin you avoid cracking may be your own!

VI. Performance Pattern. Try to consolidate and set performance pattern during these rehearsals. Repetition forms habits; be sure these performance habits are good ones.

The performance pattern for the stage managers will have been fully prepared if the stage manager has been conscientious in his training program during the Clearing Houses. Now he can use his time and energy to adjust and refine the pattern.

VII. Cutting Dialogue.   At technical rehearsals, if the production is complicated by many scenes, costumes, and cues, try to have the director agree to cutting out all unnecessary dialogue. By doing so, the stage manager can jump from cue to cue, using only enough dialogue to lead into the cue or time the change. A great deal of time and energy can be saved. Usually directors are agreeable to this method of conducting technical rehearsals, since the constant interruptions for adjustments militate against smooth acting performances.

VIII. Time Sheets.   The show must be timed as accurately as possible. The times of the scene changes during a technical rehearsal *must* be kept accurately. A formal printed time sheet is sometimes furnished by the management. If not, the stage manager will be expected to have a record of the following:

1. Day and date
2. Evening or matinee performance
3. Theater name and town
4. Performance number
5. Playing time of each scene or act in minutes and seconds
6. Time between scenes and acts in minutes and seconds
7. Total playing time
8. Total elapsed time (from rise of First Act curtain to end of last curtain call)
9. Number of curtain calls
10. Brief comment on quality of performance and other notes

The separate chart-on-one-sheet, listing performance times from the first run-through, should be kept up-to-date.

Another type of time sheet should be prepared in addition to the two mentioned above. This might be called the "Time-of-Day Running Schedule." It is a further breakdown of the formal time sheet and shows the time of day when elements smaller than acts or scenes occur. It might appear as follows:

8:25—Overture
8:30—Opening curtain
8:36—Dueling scene

8:38—Rain starts
8:45—JOHN's entrance
8:51—JOHN's exit
8:52—Card-playing scene begins
8:59—Card-playing scene ends
9:01—Rain stops
9:03—LUCY scene
9:05—CURTAIN, ACT I

9:15—Second Act starts
9:18—MARY & JOHN love scene
   etc.

This time schedule is valuable as a check on the playing time of various small parts of the play, and is useful to staff members who wish to time their arrival at the theater to see a particular portion of the performance. It should *not* be used by any backstage personnel as an accurate guide for preparation for cues, nor by the stage manager as the best method of determining the quality of the performance. There are too many unstable elements in all productions to allow this schedule to be accurate to the minute. It is useful to the stage manager as *one* of the elements determining performance quality, but it is primarily a yardstick of relative times.

IX. Curtain Calls. Rehearse all curtain calls. The director will establish these. Sometimes removing backings and rearranging furniture speed up the calls. The stage manager will co-ordinate this. Curtain calls are part of the performance pattern and should be established as such.

X. Orchestras. Ordinarily pit orchestras are not used at technical rehearsals, but sometimes are used at full, final dress rehearsals. If not used, the stage manager must remember to include cues to the orchestra among his others. An onstage orchestra is a production element and is included in all technical and dress rehearsals.

XI. Rest Periods. If the rehearsals are at night and will be long, plan a rest period and have refreshments brought in for everyone. (Don't neglect stage hands and others.) A half-hour spent this way will save hours lost through fatigue.

XII. Determining Number of Stage Hands. The number of stage hands to be used in performance and for the touring set-ups, performances, and taking down is determined during the initial setup and during technical and dress rehearsals. The stage manager with his on-the-scene advantage will be expected to have concrete ideas on this matter. The actual number of hands used will be decided by the company manager and the business agent of the Stage Hands Union Local at the place of the first setup and performances. Others consulted will be the house crew heads, the production crew heads, and the stage manager.

Understaffing, presuming the local business agent is asleep (which he is not!), is poor economy. Inefficient backstage conditions result in poor morale, which, in turn, is reflected in poor performance. Also, the chance of accident is increased. Over-staffing is as senseless in the theater as in any business and results in a shortened life for the production. A well-balanced, efficient crew should be the goal. This should be remembered: the Stage Hands Union will not object to additions to the stage crew, but it will object strenuously to attempts to reduce the crew after the minimum number has been determined. In fact, reduction of the minimum crew is never permitted unless concrete evidence of elimination or simplification of some physical elements of the production is submitted. During the technical and dress rehearsals, the stage manager, in conjunction with the production crew heads, submits to the producer, director, and designer a maximum number of suggestions for eliminations or simplifications of elements of the physical production.

Once determined, the minimum crew call is sent to the Stage Hands Union Local in each city to be played by means of the "yellow card." The yellow card, so named because of its color, is a card of three sections furnished by the local secretary of the

Stage Hands Union to the production's head carpenter. One section is filled out and sent to the local secretary at the next stand; another section is mailed to the general business office of the IA; the third section is retained by the production carpenter and is delivered by him to a representative of the union at the next stand. The card conveys this information: the name of the production crew heads and the number of production hands in each department; the number of local stage hands needed in each department to take in the production, run the performance, put out the production, and to load and unload the baggage cars. The stage manager will not handle the stage hands' yellow card, but he must know the information it contains.

PHOTOGRAPHING THE PRODUCTION

A preliminary meeting of photographer, press agent, director, designers, company manager, and stage manager should be held to plan:

1. The time and place to take the pictures
2. The number, type, and subject of the pictures to be taken

Using the information obtained at the above meeting, a shooting schedule should be composed which will take into consideration the following:

1. Eliminate unnecessary moving of camera (long and short shots)
2. Eliminate unnecessary changing of scenery
3. Eliminate unnecessary changing of costumes
4. Make quick use of and dismiss seldom used or not used actors and other personnel

The schedule itself is a list of the pictures in shooting sequence and includes:

1. Name of the picture (indicative dialogue or business)
2. Type of shot (long, medium, or close-up)
3. Actors required for each picture
4. A reminder after each picture of actors free to make costume change, or no longer needed and ready for dismissal

A copy of the schedule is provided the director, the photographer, the press agent, and the stage manager.

Company picture calls made during the rehearsal period are a part of rehearsal hours. If calls are made after an out-of-town or New York opening, and are held after a performance, they must not exceed three hours from the time of the final curtain.

PART FOUR

Managing the Performance

BEFORE THE OPENING CURTAIN

1. The acting company should be called to the theater in the afternoon or early evening for a rehearsal when it is known that an understudy will appear. Reporting to the theater early is also advisable if new dialogue is being inserted or elaborate notes on the performance are to be given.

2. All stage managers should be in the theater before the half-hour call, under any circumstances.

3. Before the house curtain has been lowered and the auditorium opened to the audience, have:

    a) The front lights and footlights been checked?

    b) All sound effects been tested?

4. *The Half-hour Call*

    a) Are all actors and understudies in the theater? If not, start locating them immediately. Here is an instance for which an up-to-date address list is necessary.

        There are many ways of making the half-hour and other calls and checking the actors. In some productions a check-in list is posted on the call board, and the actor is expected to register his arrival. Some theaters have elaborate signal systems to each dressing room. Most managers prefer to have the call made by an assistant, who personally checks the presence of each actor. Just as mechanical cuing systems are subject to failure, mechanical calling systems have their drawbacks too. The personal method of making calls assures the stage manager that the actor is in the theater, because the assistant *sees* him; assures him that the actor knows that the call has been made, because a manager has *personally told him.*

b) If any actor is missing, advise the understudy and all other actors immediately.

c) See that all visitors leave the backstage area at this time.

Sometimes there are visitors backstage who are there for legitimate reasons. An artist, sketching the backstage elements of the production while it is in progress, is an example. Be sure that all actors understand why this visitor is there. A stranger in the wings has the same effect on an actor as someone peering over his shoulder while he is writing a personal letter.

d) After checking in, no actor should leave the backstage area without permission from the stage manager.

e) Check the setting of the first scene. Check to see that all doors, windows, drapes, etc. function properly. Check all properties for the first scene and, in so far as it is possible, all props that can be preset or prepared for ensuing scenes.

f) Give notes on the performance, that may have been received during the day, to the actors. If possible, these notes will be given during the day. If the notes require considerable study and rehearsing, the actors should be called to the theater sufficiently before the half-hour call to accomplish the change. Be sure *all* personnel concerned with the change are acquainted with it.

5. *The Fifteen-minute Call*

a) If an actor is still missing and unaccounted for, make definite arrangements for the understudy to go on. Be sure all actors are alerted to the situation.

Advise the company and house managers, and arrange

that an announcement to the audience be made at the proper time. The stage manager usually makes this announcement himself. By contract between Actors' Equity and the manager, the stage manager is responsible for seeing that an announcement about understudy replacements is made before the opening curtain. Failure to make an announcement can lead to embarrassing consequences, and the stage manager will be held accountable.

For emergency understudy appearances the announcement is made personally by the stage manager before the house curtain or over a PA system. If the actor's absence is to be prolonged, the program may be changed or slips announcing the understudy may be inserted in the program. A sign at the box office is *not* a legal announcement.

It is wise to advise the stage crew that an understudy will be on. The crew can be helpful during the shifts, in the arrangement of properties, and in all technical matters.

b) Receive information concerning exact time to start the performance. Heavy rainstorms and other elements delay the arrival of audiences, and it is usually advisable to postpone starting beyond the scheduled time.

c) Start the orchestra (if any) playing the overture. The exact time to start is determined by the length of the overture, as decided previously.

6. *The Five-minute Call*

(As the five-minute call and the starting of the overture often coincide, sometimes the word "overture" is called.

It is customary to check with the production's star before making the five-minute call. It is easy to postpone the opening curtain at this point. Any delay or stalling, once the five-minute-to-opening-curtain sequence has been started, will be difficult.)

a) All first-scene actors should report to the stage, and all beginners should go onto the set. Everyone except beginners should be cleared from the set.

b) All necessary stage hands, particularly house electrician and curtain men, should stand by.

c) Check first-scene lighting, except foots and front lights.

d) Final check, using performance check list.

e) Ring the lobby signal (act-warning bell).

f) Receive permission from the company manager to start. Usually necessary only when curtain has been delayed.

g) At the proper time start the performance. The type of production and the stage manager's preferences will alter the procedure, but the following is standard:

(Commands are given orally when possible.)

(1) WORK LIGHTS OUT (to house electrician)

This is a signal that the performance is about to start and that QUIET must be maintained.

(2) FOOTS SET (to production electrician)

Electrician answers, "Foots set."

(3) HOUSE TO HALF (to house electrician)

Electrician answers, "House at half" after reaching the half-mark.

The house lights are held at the half-mark for a short time to allow last-minute seating of the audience.

This can be the cue for the orchestra to finish the overture.

At this point the announcement of understudy appearances may be made.

(4) HOUSE OUT (to house electrician)

Electrician answers, "House out" when they are.

Be sure orchestra has stopped playing.

(5) READY ON STAGE (directly to actors onstage)

(6) CURTAIN UP (to curtain men)

The production electrician takes the rising of the curtain as his cue to dim up the front lights. If he cannot see the curtain rise or hear it, a special signal should be furnished him.

Usually the only signal among the above which cannot be given orally is the curtain signal. The curtain in many theaters operates from the fly floor or pin rail, and the theater furnishes a signal light for cuing purposes.

Standard operation of a light-cue system for the beginning or ending of an act is: Light ON—READY; Light OFF—Curtain UP (or DOWN). For curtain calls: Light ON—Curtain UP; Light OFF—Curtain DOWN.

DURING THE ACT

1. Record the curtain time and all future times required by the time sheet.

2. Check lighting, including front lights and foots.

3. Follow the performance pattern established during rehearsals and previous performances. This includes prompting, giving all warnings and cues, checking and double-checking actors' entrances, checking properties, and warning the stage crews and orchestra that the end of the act is imminent.

It has been said that a good stage manager has a mysterious sixth sense, that during the performance he can spot trouble or errors intuitively. If the stage manager has integrated himself properly into the performance, there is nothing mysterious about his ability, and it is not an extrasensory phenomenon. Any break in tempo, any foreign noise, any missing light or property, in other words, any break in performance pattern should register immediately on the stage manager's mind. In this vein, no stage manager should ever be at a loss to know when to ring a bell or when to lower a curtain. Just as an actor will know from the pattern that has been set when to interrupt another actor or when to break into a pause, so will the stage manager know when to give his cues.

4. Signal the lowering of the curtain at the end of the act, and

call for house lights after the audience has had an opportunity to applaud or react.

At the end of an act or scene, if a change of scenery is to be made, it is customary for all departments to await a signal from the stage manager before starting the change. This is necessary because the stage manager must determine that the curtain is completely down, and that actors have cleared the stage and are not in a position to be injured. Having determined these things, the stage manager gives the signal for the change. This may be done by calling the word "Strike!" Another method is for the stage manager to delay asking for work lights until he has determined that all is in readiness for the change. The appearance of the work lights would be the signal for all departments to start the change.

BETWEEN THE ACTS

1. The stage manager supervises the change of scenery and checks all details. It is customary for each department head to advise the stage manager that his own department is "set and ready."

2. An assistant calls the ensuing act and sees that the proper actors come to the stage. If the change is made easily and quickly, the call is made after the change. The actor should reach the stage in time to get prepared, but unnecessary waiting around should be avoided. If the change is complicated and takes the complete intermission, the assistant can time his call to the progress of the change. In this way he keeps the actors out of the way until the scenery is practically set and it is safe (literally) for the actor to come onstage. During this call the assistant can announce any special rehearsals that are being held the next day.

3. Ring the lobby signal in sufficient time to allow the audience to resume its seats.

4. Start the new act with the procedure adopted for the production.

5. Another example of performance pattern (or establishing

good performance habits) may be added here. The performance check list used by many stage managers often is inserted in the prompt script. The following has its humorous side, but it has happened far too often with disastrous results to be ignored. The stage manager, while checking onstage props, may put down his check list, which is in the prompt script, to adjust something, realize that time is short, rush offstage, ring up the curtain, and *then* discover that he has left the prompt script onstage! This can be avoided if the stage manager keeps his check list separate from his prompt script and never removes his script from his prompt desk where it belongs. Whatever method the stage manager sees fit to adopt, he must see that his habits are good ones, his performance pattern airtight.

The stage borrowed many of its methods and, consequently, its terms from the sea and from ships. "Good performance pattern" is a term that means the same thing as the borrowed term sometimes used about stage managers—"He knows how to *run his deck.*"

CURTAIN CALLS

Curtain calls show considerable variety. There are company calls, principal-actor calls, single calls, tableaux, and others. All of them must be treated as part of the performance pattern, and receive the same careful attention that other details of the performance receive.

One bit of technique in accomplishing curtain calls may be pointed out. The curtain, during the call, *apparently* stays open longer than it actually does. In practice, the stage manager gives the Curtain Up signal, then, when the curtain is several feet from its fully open position, he gives the Curtain Down signal. The time consumed by the stage hands stopping the upward movement of the curtain, overcoming inertia, and starting the curtain downward, allows the actors sufficient time to take their bows. An inexperienced stage manager may leave the curtain in its fully open position for several seconds before giving the Curtain Down signal. This results in an overlong curtain call, both for the actor and the audience.

AFTER THE FINAL CURTAIN

1. During the run of the play, no actor or understudy should leave the theater before the final curtain call unless permission has been received from the stage manager. Permanent permission to leave early is given actors who have made their last onstage appearance before the play is over and are not required in the curtain calls. Their understudies also are given permission. It is accepted practice for all personnel who have such permission to check out with the stage manager as they leave. During rehearsals and tryout weeks, no actor should leave the theater until dismissed, even after the final curtain call, because notes may be given or rehearsals planned.

2. Remind the actors, understudies, and crew of any special rehearsals, or assignments for the following day. If the next performance is a matinee, an announcement to that effect should be made throughout the backstage area.

3. Give notes to the actors concerning their performances. It is better to do this now rather than later, as the performance is fresh in everyone's mind. If changes are made, see that all concerned receive them.

UNDERSTUDY REHEARSALS

The stage manager conducts understudy rehearsals. The acting pattern for rehearsals and for the performance has been established by the director while directing the original company. The understudy must fit himself into this pattern. Mimicking the actor who created the part is not wanted. But, in so far as the understudy is physically able, he must re-create the characterization evolved by the director and the actor who originated the part. This means that the understudy will copy physical action exactly. Readings and interpretations will not be changed except by the natural voice quality of the understudy. Additions such as

"I have a little piece of business that would fit nicely here" or suggestions because the understudy "feels" that he "does this sort of thing rather well" or omissions because "I don't feel that cross" are not to be tolerated. If called upon to perform, the understudy must fit into the play as unobtrusively as possible.

When the understudies have been hired early in the rehearsal period, have attended all rehearsals and watched the direction, they will know what is expected of them. In a few instances, especially when the understudy also acts a part and cannot observe the actor he is understudying, it will be necessary for the stage manager to supply a great deal of information and direction. Even in this instance, the stage manager's job is to re-create direction, not to originate it.

The stage manager may encounter understudies, especially young and inexperienced ones, who feel that the above treatment is unnecessarily authoritarian. They will resent what they consider a limitation placed on their creative ability. There is a limitation, and the method is dictatorial. It must be. The stage manager should explain that this method is inherent in understudying and is not a special scheme of this particular producer. The method is essential for two reasons. First, the understudy will not rehearse with the actors, and so the actors will not be familiar with the understudy's possible deviations from the pattern. Second, the use of an understudy is an emergency matter, and, even if the actors were acquainted with the deviations, it would be too much to expect a company to adapt itself to these deviations on the spur of the moment. The understudy and actors usually have little or no warning before the understudy makes his appearance. It is not logical to expect fifteen actors to adapt themselves to one understudy in an emergency. It is logical to expect an understudy to prepare himself to fit into the group of fifteen.

It has been found that it is best to hold sufficient understudy rehearsals, so that each understudy can rehearse all of his parts completely at least once a week. These should be walking rehearsals, not line rehearsals. As soon as possible after the understudies are prepared, they should be given a full dress rehearsal complete with scenery, props, costumes, sound, and usually lighting.

Understudies, unlike the regular actors, rarely get an opportunity to solidify their performance before an audience in tryouts and dress rehearsals. Their work often never goes beyond the rehearsal stage. To help them prepare themselves to meet an audience, the stage manager should make provision for the understudies to watch performances. This will give them a before-an-audience point of view. Vicarious, to be sure, but useful.

COMPANY REHEARSALS

George M. Cohan is reputed to have said that periodic rehearsals of the company during the run of the play were necessary "to take out the improvements." When, weeks after the opening, one hears such remarks as, "The play seems so fresh that it is hard to realize that it has been running for months," or "I enjoyed this performance more than the opening night," the speakers are consciously or unconsciously paying the stage manager his finest compliment. It is after the opening and during the run of the play that the stage manager has his most difficult and arduous work. Keeping the production "fresh" is no easy matter.

The inanimate elements of the production, the scenery, costumes, lights, and properties, are obviously in first-class condition or they are not. Keeping them in condition may require a certain amount of time, patience, and ingenuity, but determining their condition should present no problem. Moreover, the stage manager has highly trained production crew heads at his command to accomplish any repairs and replacements necessary to keep this section of the production fresh.

On the other hand, it is the duty of the stage manager, with only occasional assistance from the director, to see that the actors keep their part of the production fresh. This is especially true during a tour, when the production is removed from the aegis of the producer and director.

An actor's primary means of expression is his emotions. In his characterization his basic thinking is done for him by the playwright. This is not meant to imply that there are not fine minds among actors. But for characterization purposes their thinking pattern is established for them by the playwright. During the rehearsal period, the actor, with the director's help, experiments and elaborates within this thinking pattern and evolves a complete characterization, which he conveys to the audience by his emotions. Consequently, by nature or choice, or because of the demands of his profession, the actor's emotions are constantly alerted and receptive to suggestion. It is to be expected that he will consciously or unconsciously receive suggestions and incorporate them into his characterization. It is the stage manager's responsibility, after the opening performance, to screen these additions.

When the playwright, director, and producer are completely satisfied with a performance, one often hears: "Freeze that—keep the show exactly like that." In a general way this is a sound admonition. But, like all generalities, it has qualifications. First, in the legitimate theater it is not possible to "freeze" all elements of a production. An obvious example is the audience. No two audiences are exactly alike because of numerous reasons, and certainly an actor's performance must adjust to the audience. Second, it is not in the nature of things to remain static. Change is far more natural. It is with these two qualifications that the stage manager is concerned.

There is little any stage manager can do about the first qualification except to keep alert to it and help the actor adjust to it. The second qualification calls for constant vigilance and is the outstanding element of the production that must be under the control of the stage manager at all times.

The majority of changes considered by the actor will be thought to be for the betterment of his characterization and, consequently, of the play. Whether they are or not the stage manager must decide. No conscious change should be made by an actor without a consultation with the stage manager, and no change of any considerable size or consequence may be made without consultation with the director. The limits of the actor's ability and his mind (they are not necessarily alike) will often guide the stage manager in his decision. If a generalization may be made at all, it might be said that a change should meet this requirement: when one first meets the change, does it immediately appear evident that the play needs the change for its own good? If it does, fine; if it does not, it generally may be discarded.

It has been presumed changes are made consciously. This is not true always. In fact, most changes are made unconsciously and intuitively. These changes are often small and may be exceedingly insidious. The stage manager must be constantly alert to them and, if they are harmful, stop them. The new change will be hard to get rid of, once it has become established.

It has been presumed, also, the stage manager has personal integrity, experience, and discernment, and is capable of sitting in judgment on changes. Should a discussion of a change be unresolved, the problem must be referred to the director and producer.

The stage manager has no more exhilarating experience in the theater than watching and being a partner in the continuing development of a good actor's characterization during the run of the play. The subtle changes that indicate a growth of understanding, meaning, and feeling are fascinating to observe and must be nurtured by patience and understanding. Much time and thought will be expended, but the experience itself is reward enough.

There is probably no more exasperating experience than to watch an inept actor, no matter how well-meaning, tamper with the characterization the playwright and director have created for him. He will be the actor requiring most thorough and tactful controlling.

It is in the nature of things that a percentage of human beings are equipped with an overabundance of prankishness or irresponsibility or just plain cussedness. Such stupidities as self-aggrandizement or "scene-stealing" at the expense of the play are not to be tolerated. When the stage manager has ascertained that a

change has been made by an actor prompted by the above unwanted motives, the actor should be brought back into line
promptly and without ceremony, just as such people are in any
well-ordered society.

And so, when need there be a company rehearsal? The answer
is, rarely, if the stage manager has been conscientious in his duties. Usually only after notes and discussions fail to get results.
The athletic team that does not respond to talks and lectures is
taken to the field and made to *do* it. So it is with an acting company.

A considerable part of the stage manager's job of keeping the
company fresh is keeping himself fresh. A resumé of the stage
manager's progress to this point may help the reader understand
how this is done.

Beginning as a manuscript and ending as a finished production
before an audience, the play has progressed through several
periods, the writing, the planning and rehearsing, the polishing,
the performing. The stage manager advances with the play
through these periods. The technical progress of the play and the
part the stage manager has in that section of the production
should be obvious by now and will not be repeated. However, it
will be advantageous to review briefly the nontechnical progress
of the stage manager, the over-all development of his integration
into the play.

The stage manager's first important period of development and
integration is during the rehearsals. By watching the director and
actors develop characterizations, by being thoroughly familiar with
stage business, by "sharing" the emotions of the actor, by knowing
the rhythms and tempos of the performance, by being in rapport
with the actor, the stage manager will grow into the play along
with the actor.

During the polishing period (the run-through, dress rehearsal,
and tryout periods), the stage manager will combine what he has
acquired in rehearsals with the technical elements of the produc-

tion and solidify his part in the performance pattern. He is now an integral part of the production, of each performance.

The stage manager stays in the performance pattern until after the New York opening and until after everyone is comfortably set in the pattern, and then he breaks free from it. Usually this is not done abruptly but over a period of several performances, during which time his assistants take over his technical part in the pattern. If the stage manager is to advance into the next period of progress, this break must be made and it must be complete.

A stage manager who does not divorce himself from the performance pattern often lands in the pitfall that besets the actor, because he will respond to the same emotional stimuli that the actor does. It has been seen that many changes in the actor's performance are intuitive, small, and insidious. If the stage manager is in the performance pattern, he will be drawn along in the same emotional stream that influences the actor and will make the same intuitive errors the actor makes. However, if he is outside the pattern, outside the influence of the stream, he can approach the period of managing the run of the play.

There will be times when he re-enters the pattern to resume his onstage duties. He re-enters the pattern in a different way when he watches a performance from the audience. The ability to shift from the subjective to objective is a quality the stage manager must have either naturally or by training, or he will be unable to manage the long-running play. Remaining in the subjective, in the performance pattern, is emotionally exhausting, and the stage manager's duties may turn into mechanical chores. If the stage manager can become objective in his approach to the production, he will not exhaust himself and will have strength to meet the job of managing the long run, a job which will become an increasingly exciting challenge.

In these few preceding pages an attempt has been made to emphasize the qualification the producer is most likely to look for in his stage manager, the ability to keep the show fresh. To be sure, the skilled workman must know his tools. Experience in summer theaters, college theaters, and other places can furnish much of the mechanics of stage managing. This handbook will help in that direction. However, with but isolated exceptions, there is no place except Broadway or a long road tour in which the stage manager is required to do his most difficult work, manage the long run. Unless a stage manager is capable of sustaining opening-night freshness, even great skill in mechanics will not save him from the epithet "button-pusher and callboy." Only the man capable of handling this important duty may be truly called a stage manager.

REPLACEMENTS IN THE ACTING COMPANY

Occasionally actors withdraw from a company that has been running some time and will probably continue its run. A replacement must be found. Normally the producer, director, and playwright select the replacement, but sometimes the stage manager is given the job. As much thought and care should go into the selection of a replacement as into the original casting. Reference to the alternates on the original Cast List (see page 21) should be helpful. Also the advantage of having kept the actors file up-to-date should be obvious.

If the replacement is a star or featured actor in the New York company, the director usually handles the rehearsals. The stage manager often conducts rehearsals for small-part replacements. On the road the stage manager usually rehearses all replacements.

The stage manager will be guided by the director's original direction and the pattern that has been established. Stage business and the general characterization should not be altered. Minor changes due to fundamental personality differences between the original actor and the replacement must be expected. Also, as the replacement will rehearse with the regular members of the company, a greater latitude may be given the replacement than the understudy, especially if the replacement is a star. However, the stage manager's primary aim is to install the replacement with ease and comfort and as unobtrusively as possible.

The stage manager sometimes works alone with the replacement or utilizes understudies during the early rehearsals, when establishing stage business is the primary goal. However, when work on characterization starts, the actual company must be used. Obviously, understudies will not be used for rehearsals involving a star or featured-player replacement unless the star so requests, although private rehearsals with the stage manager are useful timesavers. Likewise, one cannot expect to use the acting company during all rehearsals of a very minor character. Nevertheless, all replacements have a right to a full dress rehearsal with the acting company before their first public performance.

DAILY AND WEEKLY CHECK LISTS

1. Is the address list up-to-date?
2. Are time sheets in order?
3. Have the weekly bills of the department crew heads been checked, OK'd, and handed on to the company manager? The company manager will determine day to be submitted.
4. Are the understudies completely prepared?
5. Is the acting company in good shape? Have you watched each scene *from the audience* at least once this week?
6. How are the scenery, lights, props, costumes, sound? Fresh? In good repair?
7. Have you and your assistants shifted jobs recently, so that each assistant may see the show from the audience?
8. Have you a list of actors available as replacements in case of emergencies? (If flu of epidemic proportions hits your company, what happens if you run out of understudies?)
9. Have you filed all accident reports, whether or not the services of a doctor were required? (Forms furnished by manager.)

10. Do you know how to obtain the services of the house physician quickly?
11. Have you caught up on the sleep you lost during rehearsals?

PART FIVE

Touring

This Part supplements sections on the out-of-town tryout and the setup in Part Three and applies chiefly to the long road tour.

PREPARATION FOR THE TOUR

I. Simplifying the Physical Production. During the New York run the stage manager will be planning simplifications of the physical production for the road tour. The acting company usually remains as it is in New York, but very often a large number of the physical elements of the production can be eliminated or simplified. The changes will be more in the nature of stream-lining than complete amputations. Production values must be retained. A traveler on his first trip often takes many more things than he needs. His second trip will see his luggage reduced. It is a similar attitude toward trimming production elements that governs the production staff. In an effort to insure the success of his new play, the producer may overload the New York company with extra or overelaborate production elements. Many of these elements will be found to have no essential production value and, although they are retained in New York because they are there, may be removed for a touring show.

The stage manager and production crew heads instigate most suggestions for simplification as their on-the-spot contact with the production offers them the greatest opportunity to discover them. As the line between elements that enrich a production rather than overload it is very fine, their suggestions are submitted to the producer, director, and designer for discussion and approval well in advance of the date of the projected tour.

II. Timesavers. The term "short cut" has been avoided because it connotes slipshod or skimpy methods and practices. However, short cuts that save time without in any way reducing efficiency or depriving the show of its full production values should be discovered and utilized. Alert production crew heads will have suggestions, particularly for the setup period. The stage manager should find others. Many timesavers can be planned and prepared before the tour starts. Others will be discovered as the tour progresses.

Methods of lighting the show quickly are useful, because often too much time is expended needlessly on this production element. The physical nature of the setup will determine, in part, the stage manager's method, but the lighting will be an accurate reproduction of the original.

Sometimes it is considered necessary for the scenery to be set and work lights put out before lighting can start. During the original lighting of the show that was true, but now the stage manager is reproducing the lighting, not creating it. If he must wait for the scenery, much time is wasted; and, once he does start, the other departments cannot work, because there is no light! Any scheme or short cut for overlapping activity without hurting the production will be a valuable timesaver.

A play composed of interior settings will depend on the equipment on the first pipe for most of its lighting. If the following preparations are made after the original lighting has been completed, most of the instruments can be focused at the next setup, while they are being mounted on the pipe, which will be near the floor for easy access.

1. Get exact height of pipe from floor when in position.

2. Make permanent arrangements, so that relation of pipe to portal is always the same.

3. Mark on the pipe the exact position of each instrument's hanger or clamp.

4. Mark each instrument as follows:

   a) Number of position on pipe
   b) Alignment marks on clamp and arm to set stage L. or R. direction
   c) Alignment marks on instrument and hanger arm or yoke to set tilt of instrument
   d) Mark focus.

If all instruments are in their proper places on the pipe when mounted by men working at floor level and individual alignment marks are correct, then they should be in position when the pipe is raised and properly adjusted to the portal. Only minor adjustments, if any, will be needed. Moreover, this focusing can be done while full work lights are on, while other departments are using most of the stage, and before, during, or after the scenery (except the portal, which is usually the first thing up anyway) is set up.

The above method of saving time should not be construed as being the best or only possible scheme. It is a sample, that's all. However, this type of short cut eliminates nothing but time and is valuable. All departments should be scrutinized for such possible timesavers. Short cuts that eliminate lighting instruments, scenery, properties, costumes, and, consequently, production values should not be resorted to except in emergency and then should be in the nature of planned emergency simplification.

III. Emergency Simplification. Emergencies arise in spite of the most careful planning and preparation for a tour. After the advance agent has checked the stage and delivered the hanging plot and other advices, the stage house may be altered structurally, and no one bother to tell the touring company before it arrives. Hemp lines may be old, but no one has taken the trouble to check them. Traps may be cut incorrectly. Movie sound horns and screens should have been removed, but are not. Also delayed trains cause late arrival in a town, and valuable time is lost. Methods of eliminating valuable elements in the physical production should be considered for such emergencies. The stage manager and production crew heads will discuss what emergency steps can be taken and will plan their execution.

Time saved by simplification of the setup may prevent cancellation or delayed start of a performance. Time saved in the taking down and loading out may prevent missing a train. Eliminating platforms, staircases, cornices, baseboards, wainscoting, backings, and ceilings may be considered in the scenery department. Eliminating a single piece of furniture will save time, if one realizes the time it takes to remove it from the baggage car, unpack it from its crate, unwrap it from its padded covers, and then, after the performance, to repad it, recrate it, and reload it into the baggage car. Most eliminations will come in the carpentry and property departments, as eliminations in the other departments bring too many complications. Leaving out a few lighting instruments might mean such a complete new switchboard hookup that the time consumed plotting and understanding the new hookup would be greater than the time saved by not hanging the instruments. Generally sound effects cannot be eliminated, nor can costumes.

After being determined, these emergency simplifications should be discussed with the actors so that they are familiar with the changes that will be made in the performance pattern. Very often elimination of a physical element of the production brings dialogue and stage business changes.

No emergency simplification should be resorted to for any reason other than the planned one. Reducing the production because of "convenience" or laziness should not be permitted. Podunk must see as complete a physical production as Broadway, all things being equal.

IV. Preparing the Acting Company. Many actors have had touring experience, but there may be some in the company who have not. The stage manager will advise them of what they may expect and what is required of them.

A. THE CALL. The material found in Part Three of this handbook should be brought to the attention of the company.

B. TRAVELING. Although the crew, the stage manager, and others may "travel ahead," *all actors travel with the company at all times.* The producer is the only one who may make an exception to this rule.

C. HOTELS. The discussion on hotel reservations in Part Three should be reviewed.

D. TRUNKS. In addition to the information in Part Three, the company should know that during one-night stands hotel trunks are not delivered daily but are left in the baggage car, if the same car will be used for the next move, or are stored during the day by the transfer company. However, hotel trunks must be *available* to the actors *at least once every week,* even during one-night stands. This is usually accomplished on the day when a theater with an unusually large stage is to be played. The hotel trunks are brought to the theater, not delivered to hotels, because some actors may not have a hotel reservation for that one day. The trunks are put in an out-of-the-way place where the actors will have access to them without disrupting the production. Theater trunks must be brought to the theater daily.

E. HAND LUGGAGE. Hand luggage is the individual's personal responsibility, and he will be expected to handle it as he sees fit. Personnel inexperienced in touring should be advised that they will be wise to keep hand luggage to a minimum. Today trains are crowded, and red-caps and taxis scarce. This is especially true on Sundays and at late hours, the normal traveling day and time for a touring company.

F. REHEARSALS. The actors should realize that regular understudy and any necessary company rehearsals will be held during the tour just as they are in New York.

G. SICKNESS. It is even more important that the management be kept advised of the health of the actor while he is on tour than when he is in New York.

H. SIMPLIFICATIONS AND EMERGENCIES. The stage manager will discuss and rehearse with the actors all planned emergency simplifications that he and the crew heads have decided upon. This may mean cutting or transposing dialogue, rearranging stage business, and so on.

ON ARRIVAL AT THE NEW STAND

The stage manager will inspect the theater as soon as he can. He is the one who will decide what emergency or other simplification is necessary, if any.

There are many small things the stage manager can do to smooth out the arrival of the rest of the company, when he is traveling ahead with the crew.

He can advise the taxi-starter at the railroad station of the time that the company is arriving and the number of passengers he may expect.

He can check hotel reservations to see that they are being held. This is particularly important if the company is arriving by a late train and may mean that more desirable rooms are held.

He can check the position and spelling of names on the theater marquee. Errors can be corrected before the actors see them.

He can confirm appointments with newspaper or radio people. It has happened that stage managers have filled in on a radio program when the company is delayed, rather than lose valuable air time.

There may be other things he will do. However, his first duty is at the theater, seeing that the setup is under way and progressing satisfactorily.

LOADING IN, OR THE NEW SETUP

The following terms mean:

> *Load* (or *Take*) *In*—Transferring the production from the baggage cars or from a storehouse or just from a truck and putting it into the theater
>
> *Set Up*—Assembling the production in the theater for a performance

Take Down—Dismantling the production and preparing it
for transportation

Load (or *Put*) *Out*—Transferring the production from the
theater and into the baggage cars

However, as loading in and setting up are almost continuous
or simultaneous operations at most touring stands, the terms
are used interchangeably. Likewise with taking down and
loading out.

There are times when all four terms are applicable. E.g., over
a week end the production may be loaded in on Sunday with
the setup on Monday. The following Saturday night the production might be taken down, and then on Sunday it would
be loaded out.

The stage manager will be at the theater at the appointed hour
for the call and will be in attendance throughout the setup. His
duties include:

I. Dressing Rooms.   He will assign and personally check all
dressing rooms, toilets, and other facilities. He will check that
trunks and costumes are properly distributed. The posted dressing room list should include a reminder of matinee days, and half-
hour and curtain times, all of which may change from city to city.

II. Answering Questions.   No two stage houses are alike, and
so problems will arise. He will answer questions and make decisions.

III. Prompt Desk.   He will place the prompt desk and check
all cuing devices, including fixed equipment belonging to the
theater. He will establish with the house electrician a half-mark
for the house lights and the routine used for opening and closing
each act.

IV. Lighting.   He will light the show quickly and accurately.

V. Curtains.   Because of its weight or rigging, the house curtain may be easy or difficult to operate, slow or fast. With the
actual men who will operate the curtain during the performance,
the stage manager will test and rehearse the speed of the curtain.
Some people's reaction time is slower than others. This rehearsal

gives the stage manager an opportunity to time the curtains exactly. The curtain men should be advised of the number of curtain calls normally taken and when they are taken. Usually curtain calls come after the final act, but in some productions, especially revivals of stylized plays, there are curtain calls after other acts.

VI. Interviewing and Rehearsing Extras. After the stage manager has experienced two or three moves and their consequent setups, he should have a fairly accurate time schedule established. He will arrange that the call for interviewing extras and the time allotted for their costuming and rehearsing do not interfere with other departments. Very often the rehearsal can be accomplished during the stage crew run-through.

VII. Stage Crew Run-through. A run-through for the technical departments will be held, if advisable. Normally, a technical rehearsal with the actors present is not necessary.

VIII. Time Sheet. The stage manager will supply the house crew heads with the running time of the show, by acts and scenes. He will warn them of quiet scenes and other production specialties to be alert to.

IX. Orchestra. He will meet with the orchestra leader and discuss music and cuing.

X. Performance Pattern. He will take notes on any variation to the performance pattern and will advise all personnel concerned.

XI. Acoustics. Test the acoustics of the theater for voices. Test theater-furnished PA systems, especially if used in conjunction with production-furnished electronic sound equipment.

DURING THE TOURING STAND

I. Keeping in Touch. Keep the New York production office advised concerning the show via time sheets or other methods.

II. Address List. Be sure that the company manager and all assistant stage managers have a copy of the new address list for each city. If the address list is combined with the personnel check-off list, be sure the above people know who are traveling ahead and who are traveling with the company.

It is good practice to post on the call board of each stand the local addresses and phone numbers of the company manager and all stage managers.

III. Hotels. Keep hotel information for future stands available for all. Sometimes the advance agent deals directly with the stage manager in matters pertaining to hotel reservations. Other times he relays the information through the company manager. In any event the actors will look to the stage manager for advice about hotels, and he will do all he can to assist them.

IV. Trunks. Prepare a new hotel trunk pickup list for this stand and a delivery list for the next stand.

V. Rehearsals. The stage manager will find out local rules governing understudy and/or company rehearsals on the stage, the use of lights, props, and other facilities. Managing to find time for understudy rehearsals during a tour is always a problem, but they must not be neglected. A wise stage manager defers to the understudies if a time most congenial to the majority is suggested.

VI. Anticipating Change in Performance Pattern. The stage manager will anticipate changes in the performance pattern for the next stand. E.g., the Erlanger in Buffalo has a very peculiarly shaped and crowded Offstage Right area. Further complications arise, because all entrances from the dressing rooms to the stage are made through a door in the Downstage Rightstage wall. Knowing these things in advance will help the stage manager plan necessary performance pattern changes.

Problems will be presented not only by small stages but by over-large stages (Des Moines), unique dressing room arrangements (Forrest, Philadelphia), raking stages (Baltimore), special electric current (Providence, formerly, maybe elsewhere now), flooring downstage laid on concrete, traps impossible (Kansas City), and so on.

The problems to be met at well-known theaters can be solved

weeks in advance. The advance agent will keep the company posted on stage conditions. Further advice may be received from the production crew heads and from actors who have made recent tours.

If necessary, rehearsals of performance pattern changes should be held at a previous stand while there is leisure time, rather than waiting until the new stand's setup day.

VII. Actors File. It has happened that emergencies in the acting company arise for which the planned understudy coverage (even double-cover) is not sufficient. Most stage managers keep a personal file of actors for such contingencies. The New York office will have replacement actors in mind; but, when you are in St. Paul, New York is pretty far away.

This personal actors file often is composed of actors the stage manager knows who live in the area where the show is playing or actors he has met during the tour. While playing large cities, the stage manager frequently is visited by actors seeking employment. If they seem likely prospects, the stage manager can sound them out for willingness to act temporarily in such an emergency. Quite obviously these actors can be used in small parts only and must be good studies. If the emergency occurs in St. Paul or Des Moines or Omaha, a call to Chicago can produce an actor in a couple of hours, whereas a New York replacement might not arrive in time to prevent cancellation of a performance.

Most cities large enough to support a road show will have very capable radio, television, or university and little-theater actors available for such emergencies.

It must be understood that the situation described is an *extreme* emergency, one that threatens to close the show. No production, touring or otherwise, should be running without competent and complete understudy coverage.

VIII. Co-operation. Touring is a co-operative venture for all concerned, particularly for the company and stage managers. The actual mechanics of moving from city to city, the business end of the theater, are in the provinces of the company manager and the advance agent. However, in his role of liaison staff member, the stage manager will work in close association with the front of the house and will be called upon to assist and give advice in many problems. The stage manager is in the best position to know the interests, the community pulse, of backstage personnel, and so he will be expected to make suggestions for their welfare. To make suggestions intelligently, it behooves the stage manager to have a knowledge of the duties and problems that face the company manager and the advance agent. From suggesting train times to counting up, if the company manager is ill; from relaying information about appointments to filling in when an actor cannot get to an appointment, will be problems that may face the stage manager.

When the stage manager travels ahead, he and the company manager exchange some of their duties. The stage manager may help the company manager by doing certain routine front-of-the-house matters before the company manager arrives. While the stage manager is ahead of the others, the company manager helps the assistant stage managers with company problems that may arise.

The dividing line between the front of the house and backstage is very faint in a touring company. The closer the relationship between stage manager and company manager, the more efficiently the tour will be conducted, and company morale will be higher.

LOADING OUT

I. Schedule. After the final performance the stage manager usually stays in attendance during the taking down and loading out of the production. He will check that:

a) Dismantling and loading is on schedule

b) All parts of the production are removed from the theater

c) Dressing rooms have been cleared of theater trunks, wardrobe, make-up, and any personal property of the company

II. The Call.   He will see that the Call is picked up by the carpenter or himself.

III. Traveling Ahead.   It is not unusual for the stage crew to travel to the next city on a train many hours ahead of that taken by the acting company. In fact, the setup in the new city may be under way before the company leaves the last stand. The stage manager will want to be at the new theater when the new setup starts, and so he will travel with the crew. Traveling ahead (which includes loading out, the actual trip, and the new setup) is very fatiguing work for a stage manager, because he loses meals and sleep and does not get the few respites that the stage hands do during a performance. The stage manager should train his assistants, so that traveling ahead can be alternated among the stage-managing staff. Generally the stage manager sends an assistant ahead when the theater at the next stand presents no problem or change in performance pattern.

KEEPING THE COMPANY FRESH

Just one thing can be added to what has been written about keeping the company fresh, and that is more of an extension to "Company Rehearsals" in Part Four than a distinct addition.

During the run of the play in New York, many of the personnel will have little more to do with each other outside the theater, outside business hours as it were, than the average office worker will have with his fellow workers. When the performance is over, the individuals will separate and return to their respective families and friends. This is natural since New York is the permanent home of many actors, and the paths of fellow workers need not cross. On tour the company will be thrown together almost continuously. Long train trips, living in the same hotels, eating at the same restaurants, separation from friends, few opportunities to make new acquaintances are among the factors that bring personnel together intimately. A sort of traveling community is created.

An actor's performance will be influenced by his daily life—

that should be obvious. As the stage manager is responsible for performances, he should do all in his power to make the touring-company community a happy one. Many members of the company will take advantage of each new city's parks, beaches, museums, and other points of interest. They will attend concerts and movies and sporting events. They will seek out things to do to substitute for their normal home activities. The stage manager must be alert to the personnel's extracurricular activities, as they should influence his planning of company or understudy rehearsals and other company activities.

No blanket statement can be made as to where the stage manager's solicitude for personnel should start or end. The character of the personnel in a particular company will help the stage manager determine this for himself. One point, however, should be mentioned. The producer, by signing an Equity contract with the actor, acquires exclusive right to the actor's services. Any outside employment and, as an extension of this, any outside activity that has a deleterious effect on an actor's performance will be of vital interest to the producer and, consequently, the stage manager. The producer presumes the stage manager will concern himself with an actor's outside activity in so far as the welfare of the production is affected.

CANADIAN TOURS

Extended Canadian tours are rare, but shows that include Buffalo in their itinerary often include Toronto. The manifests, bonds, and arrangements necessary to enter and leave Canada are the company manager's headache, but there are two things the stage manager will supervise.

1. Obtain a set of keys from each actor for each of his trunks, hotel and theater. Tag these keys for identification purposes and turn them over to the property man. When the company enters Canada, trunks will be examined by Canadian Customs *in the baggage car,* with usually no one but the

property man in attendance. A wise actor will retain a duplicate set of keys.

2. When the company leaves Canada to return to the States, the American Customs will furnish a representative, who will be in attendance at the theater during the last performance and during the taking-down and loading-out period. During the performance he will assist the actors and other personnel in preparing their individual customs declarations. The stage manager can assist by routing actors to this representative when they have leisure time. During the loading-out period, the customs man will examine all actors' theater trunks, all wardrobe department trunks, hampers, prop boxes, etc., etc., before they are closed, will supervise locking them, and will affix a seal. Hotel trunks, which will have been picked up previously, will have been examined before the last performance in the presence of the property man, and will have been sealed into the baggage car.

If there are alien actors in the company, the company manager will handle the details of clearing them for entrance to and return from Canada *with the company and at the proper time*. The stage manager must impress on these aliens that care should be taken when playing border cities. A sight-seeing tour of Niagara Falls with a short visit across the International Bridge just "to see the view" can turn into a prolonged stay as a guest of Immigrations!

STAGE MANAGER'S EQUIPMENT

During the tour the stage manager will need a certain amount of equipment and supplies. It can be seen that he is constantly preparing new trunk, dressing room, and other lists. A typewriter is practically indispensable. Also, he will need, in varying degrees of importance and frequency, paper, carbons, thumbtacks, scotch tape, pencils, erasers, a supply of time sheets, extra manuscripts, extra parts, chalk, envelopes, stamps, clipboards, scratch pads, pencil sharpeners, scissors, ruler, tape, paper clips, paper fasteners, a stapler, ink, colored pencils, first-aid kit. Ingenious work boxes have been devised to accommodate these supplies. On the other hand, they can be wrapped in an old newspaper and tucked away in an empty corner of a property or lighting crate. In a small production having practically no cues, a stage manager can get along with almost nothing, not even the traditional music stand to hold his prompt script. In a heavy production, the stage manager usually has equipment of his choice carried with the production to guarantee adequate and standard prompt-desk facilities. In this matter, as in all others, the stage manager will choose his own method of how to accomplish his duties.

THE END OF THE TOUR

Eventually the show closes, either temporarily or permanently. If the closing is temporary, the producer will store the production intact or practically so. Preparing the production for storage is a co-operative task for the production crew heads, the company manager, and the stage manager, based on directives from the producer.

I. Temporary Closing. Lighting and sound equipment is usually rented. It is returned to the owner after complete lists and special notes have been made, so that the equipment can be reassembled or replaced exactly. The scenery, props, and costumes are inventoried, packed, and stored as directed by the producer.

Packing is handled by the production crew heads, who take precautions against damage by the elements, bad handling, moths, etc.

Inventories and lists are compiled by the production crew heads, prepared in at least triplicate by the stage manager (he has the typewriter!), collected and organized by the company manager, and then turned over to the producer.

All containers—crates, boxes, trunks, bundles—are numbered and labeled, and a master list is compiled as a record. Each container has its individual label and packing lists, one list inside the container and the other affixed to the outside. The third copy of the list is collected, with the inventories, for the producer, and a notation of the place of storage is made on it. These inventories and packing lists give the producer exact knowledge of the whereabouts of any and all production elements.

The remainder of the production—personnel, manuscripts, stationery, time sheets, and personal trunks—is brought to New York City. Trunks are delivered as requested; the rule for delivering in New York City is the same as that for collecting. (See Part Three.) Manuscripts, etc. are collected by the stage manager and delivered to the producer. A final address list of all personnel is compiled.

II. Closing Permanently.   When a show closes on the road, lighting and sound equipment, personnel and personal trunks, manuscripts and time sheets will be brought to New York City as they are for a temporary closing. Scenery, props, and costumes are disposed of locally, *in toto* if possible, in order to save the cost of handling and transporting to another city.

The producer usually gives considerable thought to the disposal of his production, unless the closing is sudden and unexpected. He has several alternatives—selling, giving away, destroying, or storing.

Scenery, the most valuable element, is the most difficult to sell. It is usually given away or destroyed, almost never stored. The local house carpenter may take it as a gift in order to salvage valuable stage hardware and lumber. Little theaters and other organizations sometimes will accept it but rarely have funds for paying for it. A great deal of scenery is taken to the local dump and destroyed.

Small properties of slight value are given to the taker, often the house property man. Those not taken are destroyed. Good pieces of furniture and carpeting can usually be sold for enough to warrant their transportation to New York City.

Modern costumes, especially street clothes, are sometimes bought by the actors who wear them. Secondhand clothing dealers will buy some things. Welfare or charitable organizations will welcome the opportunity to collect serviceable clothing and furniture. Period costumes are bought by costume-rental houses or may be given to little theaters, schools, or to organizations that can salvage the material in them. Wardrobe baskets and trunks, well-made property boxes and crates are brought to New York and stored for use by a future production.

By careful planning, company managers and stage managers can dispose of all elements of the production profitably, either by selling them or by giving them into the hands of a deserving organization or individual.

Appendices

A. The Manuscript as Received from the Playwright

John
Whenever I find that the . . .

(The telephone rings)

Daisy
(Picking up the phone on her desk)
John Smithers' office. Miss Caramel speaking.

(Hanson's angry voice is heard over the
phone, but the words are not distin-
guishable. Daisy holds the receiver
away from her ear, and each time Hanson
pauses for a breath Daisy tries to
speak.)

Yes, Mr. Han . . .

(Hanson has a fresh breath and goes
on talking for quite a while.)

But, if you'd just let me . . .

(Again Hanson speaks)

(John has been quietly amused with
Daisy's predicament and decides to
offer his help. He takes the phone
from Daisy and shouts into it.)

John
(Shouting)
Listen, you old bag of wind, settle down!

(Hanson continues angrily but soon quiets
down, and the audience no longer can
hear him.)

John (con't)
Fine! Fine! I'll see you tonight about eight-thirty.
(He hands the phone back to Daisy, who
replaces the receiver in its cradle.)
Hanson can drown out a brass band when he gets started. Hard on the
ears . . .
(then, slyly)
. . . especially such pretty pink ones, like yours.

(Daisy is embarrassed and, to tell
the truth, a bit apprehensive.)

Daisy
Oh, Mister Smithers!

John
(Resuming his office manner)
Yes, yes, ah . . . well, yes. I think we have time for one more letter.

Daisy
(With regained aplomb.)
Certainly, Mr. Smithers.

John
(Dictating)
"Mr. A. Brush Wallaby"
(aside to Daisy)
Put this on my personal stationery. You'll find his address in my
personal address book under Australia.
(dictating again)
"Dear Wally" comma "Long time no hear from" dash "anxious to hear how
things progress with all the supalia" period. That's . . .
(He spells it out)
. . . s - u - p - a - l - i - a . . .
(Explaining, a bit self-consciously)
you know, plural diminutive for marsupial. Ha, ha! Well, ahem, ah ...
(Resumes his dictation)
"Molly and the kids pester the life out of me asking me when . . ."

(The telephone rings again and
Daisy answers it.)

Daisy
(into telephone)
John Smithers' office, Miss Caramel speaking.
(She listens for a moment)
Why, yes, Mr. Filibuster.

(John is startled. He gesticulates wildly
that he is "not in", that he has "gone out".
At first Daisy apparently does not understand, and so, while she continues to
listen to the phone, John re-enacts that he
is "not in". We know that Daisy is just
playing a game and are not surprised when
she nods her head that she understands.
John heaves a big sigh of relief, gets his
hat from the closet, and starts out. As
he passes Daisy he pats her on the shoulder.)

(Daisy is left alone on the stage listening
to Mr. Filibuster on the phone as

The Curtain descends very, very slowly.)

ACT ONE, Scene 4

(It is shortly after eight o'clock the
evening of the same day and we find our-
selves in Harry Hanson's house, in his
own workroom and hideaway, to be exact.
This is a small but comfortable room
with well-worn chairs and with shelves
for many books. A small table-desk is
at one side, a fireplace in the wall
opposite, a door leads to the rest of
the house. Through the darkened windows
we see vivid flashes of lightning, and
the thunder fairly shakes the house.
When the curtain rises we see Harry
sitting before the flickering fire reading the evening paper. Voices are
heard from offstage, and Harry putting
aside his paper, rises as Tom Albion
and Dick Bestor enter.)

Harry

Glad to see you could make it tonight, Tom.

(They shake hands)

Tom

You know I never miss these sessions, Harry.

Harry
(To Dick Bestor)

Richard Bestor, my old college roommate and lifelong pal. Richard
Bestor. How are you, Dick?

Dick

Fine, Harry, just fine.

(They shake hands)

Harry

Make yourselves comfortable. John should be along any minute now. I
talked to him on the phone this afternoon - said he'd try to get here
by eight-thirty.

(There is a bright flash of lightning,
followed by a tremendous clap of
thunder.)

Hope this storm doesn't keep him away.

                              Dick
He hates driving in the rain.

                              Tom
I don't know that I blame him. That hill down from his house is really
treacherous during a storm.

                              Dick
We had a bad scare on it the other day when I was driving back from the
Canajoharie Country Club.

                              Harry
How did you get onto that road? We always use the Tallahassee-Spokane
Highway coming from the Club.

                              Dick
Bill Crunch's wife had their car and we were taking him home. It wouldn't
have been . . .

                    (The telephone rings)

                              Harry
                    (answering)
Yes?
                    (He listens)
Oh, hello, Molly . . .

                    (Voices are heard offstage)

Just a second, Molly . . .
                    (He listens to the voices)
You don't have to worry, he just arrived.

                    (John enters)

                              Harry (con't)
                    (into phone)
One minute and I'll put him on.
                    (Hands phone to John)
It's Molly, John.

                              John
                    (into phone)
Hello, dear.
                    (He listens)
Now just relax and take it easy - I'll be OK.
                    (Listens. Harry signals him that he
                     would like to say something to Molly.)
Certainly, dear, certainly. Harry wants to talk to you again.
                    (Passes phone to Harry)

                        Harry
                (into phone)
Molly, now don't you worry. This storm will be over in a halfhour . . .

                (Terrific lightning and thunder)

. . . at least I think it will be. Everything's under control. Yes . . .
yes . . . Right! Goodbye.
                (He hangs up)

                        John
Molly gets into quite a state on nights like this if I'm out in it.
Spends most of her time on the phone calling the neighbors.

                        Tom
Don't blame her. Dick was just telling us he had a bad time on that hill
of yours the other day.

                        Dick
Fortunately we were just creeping along. Even so we turned completely
around. Nothing else in sight and stayed on the road. Lucky. Glad I'm
within walking distance tonight. You too, eh, Tom?

                        Tom
You bet!

                        John
Yes, Molly worries and hangs onto the phone - does all day, anyway, storm
or no storm.

                        Harry
                (Who has been trying the radio,
                 abandons it)
Nothing but static. Drink, John?
                (He starts to mix a highball)

                        John
Not when I'm driving.

                        Harry
Wise.
                (To the others)
Drink? Oh, good, you've already helped yourselves.

                        Tom
Can't resist your bourbon, Harry.

                        Harry
                (Indicating a chair)
This suit you, John?

John

My favorite.
(picks up newspaper)
How'd the Yankees make out?

Harry

Won again. Three to one.

Dick

Poor Red Sox.

John

Williams got the only run, I see, a homer. I can't understand how such a
good team loses so many games.

(They ponder this for a moment)

Harry
(Broaching a new subject)
I've been thinking over what you suggested last week, Tom. I'm disposed
to agree that it might be a good thing for all of us.

Dick

You mean this getting-things-out-of-our-system business?

Harry

Yes. You'll remember that Tom thought that it would be beneficial to us
all. Need to unload once in a while. Bad for us to keep anything bottled
up too long. I'm all for it. How about the rest of you?

Tom

Obviously I'm for it or I would never have mentioned it.

Dick

I'll tag along. How about you, John?

John

Well, I . . .

Harry
(Quickly, overriding any objection)
Of course John's with us. Tom, as it was your suggestion, how about you
taking the lead?

Tom

Right. I've kept this quiet, as I guess you have the things you'll tell
us. I gamble. Oh, not just a tenth of a cent at bridge - I really gamble
dice, roulette, cards - the works. Fortunately no one at the bank knows
it and fortunately gambling with other people's money doesn't interest me.
Also, I can afford it. But the strain of keeping it under my hat has been

Tom (con't)

terrific. Glad to share it.

(A pause while they ponder Tom's trouble)

Your turn, Dick.

Dick
(Blurting it out)
I drink! Of course you've seen me take a drink or two at a party or like
this. I don't mean that. About twice a year I go up to the cabin with a
case or two of whiskey and just soak it in. I don't shave or bathe - in
fact I'm just a sodden mass - a fine looking surgeon! After about a week
I've had enough and I get straightened out and that's that for another six
months. I hate it but there it is. Now you, too, know.

(Another pause)

Harry
You men have been frank and so shall I. It's women with me.

(Astonishment shows on their faces)

Yes, you can stare. Harry Hanson, pillar of the church, the perfect family
man with a lovely wife, fine children. I know what people think and say
about me and they might not believe this but it's true. I, too, periodically go off the track. I go to the Big City, hide away in a hotel and
have women. A series of them. After it's over, I return to my family, my
wife, whom I love dearly, and never think of another woman, not for many
months. And there you have it!

(Another pause)

Well, John, it's up to you.

John
(John has a strange look on his face -
he seems to be transported to another
world. He speaks with difficulty.)
No. I'm afraid . . . no, I better not.

Tom
Come, come. It'll do you good.

John
No. It's too terrible. You'll all hate me. You'll never speak to me
again.

Harry
You know we all agreed. Certainly you'll tell us. Why, see how much
better we all feel. Come on, now.

John

Well, if you really think . . .

Dick

It's the best thing.

John

If you'll promise . . .

(The others, simultaneously)

Tom	Dick	Harry
Certainly!	Of course!	Naturally, naturally!

John

It's like this. I'm a terrible gossip and I just can't wait to get home to tell my wife everything.

(Consternation reigns among the others)

The Curtain Falls

ACT ONE, Scene 5

                    (The following morning. We are back in
                    John Smithers' office. When the curtain
                    rises Daisy is at her desk, busy sorting
                    the morning mail. After a moment or two
                    John enters.)

                              John
                    (Going to closet and hanging up his hat)
Good morning, Miss Caramel.

                              Daisy
                    (Making each dimple more attractive)
Good morning, Mr. Smithers!

                              John

Got the mail sorted?

                    (Daisy hands him the mail)

Good.
                    (He sits at his desk and opens his
                    letters. He reads one hurriedly and
                    passes it to Daisy.)
Just a short note answering this. The usual "sorry, conditions won't
permit further expansion at this time."
                    (Picks up another letter)
Well, well. Good thing we never finished that letter yesterday, Miss
Caramel. Here's one from ... ha, ha ... "supalia" ... ha, ha!

                              Daisy

Oh, how fortunate.

                    (The telephone rings - Daisy answers)

                              Daisy
John Smithers' office, Miss Caramel speaking.
                    (She listens)
He's right here, Miss Lammerton.
                    (She listens)
Certainly. Yes, I'll tell him.
                    (She hangs up)
                    (To John)
That was Miss Lammerton, Dr. Richard Bestor's office nurse. Dr. Bestor
won't be able to have lunch with you today. He left town suddenly and
won't be back for two weeks.

                    John
Oh?

                    Daisy
He went to his camp.

                    John
          (With a speculative gleam)
Ohhh?

          (Daisy returns to her desk)

          (John is lost in happy thought. His
          far-away look settles on Daisy and a
          new idea comes to him.)

                    John
Miss Caramel . . .

                    Daisy
Yes, Mr. Smithers?

                    John
Miss Caramel, has Mr. Harry Hanson ever

          etc.   etc.

B. The Stage Manager's Working Prompt Script

Warnings and cues are marked in color. For the purpose of reproduction in black and white, the following symbols for colors will be used:

RED (Sound)	———————————
BLUE (Actors)	— — — — — — — — — —
GREEN (Lights)	. . . .
BROWN (Scenery)	—.—.—.—.—.—

JOHN X upstg, then
back, picks up phone ∧base,
X down, then to desk

WARN
END
ACT

John

Whenever I find that the . . .

PHONE

(PHONE)

Daisy
(picks up phone on her desk)
John Smithers' office. Miss Caramel speaking.

SOUND #9

(HANSON'S voice heard over phone.
DAISY holds receiver away from ear
and each time HANSON pauses
DAISY tries to speak)

Yes, Mr. Han . . .

(HANSON again)

But, if you'd just let me . . .

(HANSON again)

(JOHN quietly amused picks up his
extension from his desk and takes
charge.)

John

Listen, you old bag of wind, settle down!

(DAISY replaces her phone - starts
writing)

(HANSON continues angrily, soon
quiets down)

WARN
PHONE

(JOHN rises, listens, paces)

Fine! Fine! I'll see you tonight about eight-thirty.
(HE replaces phone, Xes to L. of
Daisy)
Hanson can drown out a brass band when he gets started. Hard
on the ears . . .
(slyly)
especially such pretty pink ones, like yours.

Daisy
(embarrassed, looks at desk)
Oh, Mister Smithers!

(SITS)

1 - CURTAIN
2 - WORK LIGHTS
3 - PORTAL OUT
4 - TABLE TURN
5 - PORTAL IN
6 - START RAIN
7 - WORK LIGHTS OUT
8 - CURTAIN UP
9 - FLASH

                    John
            (resuming office manner, Xes to
            his chair)
Yes, yes, ah . . . well, yes. I think we have time for one
more letter.

                    Daisy
            (dead pan)
Certainly, Mr. Smithers.
            (takes notebook from drawer, picks
            up pencil, turns to John)

                    John
            (dictating)
"Mr. A. Brush Wallaby"
            (aside to Daisy, small smile)
Put this on my personal stationery. You'll find his address
in my personal address book under Australia.
            (dictating)
"Dear Wally" comma "Long time no hear from" dash "what goes"
question mark. "Anxious to hear how things progress with all
the supalia" period. That's . . .
            (spelling)
. . . s - u - p - a - l - i - a . . .
            (explaining, self-conscious)
you know, plural diminutive of marsupial. Ha, ha! Well,
ahem, ah . . .
            (resumes dictation)
"Molly and the kids pester the life out of me asking me when . .

        (PHONE)

                                        PHONE
            (DAISY answers, puts down notebook,
            turns front)

                    Daisy
            (into phone)
John Smithers' office. Miss Caramel speaking.
            (listens a moment)
Why, yes, Mr. Filibuster.

            (JOHN startled rises, Xes D.C., turns
            to Daisy, gestures wildly that he is
            "not in" has "gone out". DAISY pre-
            tends not to understand continues to
            listen to phone. JOHN re-enacts "not
            in" bus. SHE nods she understands.
            JOHN smiles, gets hat from closet,   stet
            starts out, pats Daisy's shoulder
            head on way. DAISY alone listens to Filibuster)

                    MEDIUM CURTAIN

Between scenes Sound Cue #10,
Record #11, "Filibuster's Voice," over
Front Speakers.

At RISE:
    ON: HARRY
    OFF: TOM
           DICK
           JEEVES
    READY: JOHN

READY   THUNDER
             LIGHTNING

ACT ONE, Scene 4

(Shortly after eight the same evening.
Harry Hanson's workroom and hideaway.)

L & T
Vol. 1

(AT RISE: HARRY sits in chair U.S. of
fireplace, reading newspaper)

                    Tom (offstage)
What a storm!

          (HARRY looks up)

                    Jeeves (off)
Very wet, sir. Yes, sir.

                    Dick (off)
Better put those coats in the kitchen, Jeeves.

          (HARRY puts paper in chair, rises,
          Xes C.)

                    Jeeves (off)
Yes, sir.

          (TOM ALBION and DICK BESTOR enter
          through door)

TOM
DICK

*WARN
PHONE*

                    Harry
Glad you could make it tonight, Tom.

          (THEY shake hands)

                    Tom
You know I'd never miss these sessions, Harry.
          (Xes U.L.)

                    Harry
          (mock formality)
Richard Bestor! Doctor Richard Bestor!
          (easily)
How are you, Dick, you old sawbones?
          (slaps his back)

*NEXT
PG.
L & T*

                    Dick
Fine, Harry, just fine!

          (THEY shake hands. DICK Xes to frplc)

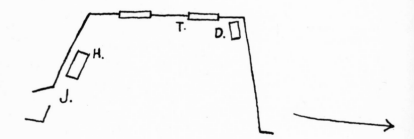

(JOHN'S ENTRANCE)

Harry

Make yourselves comfortable. John should be along any minute
now. I talked to him on the phone this afternoon - said he'd
try to get here by eight-thirty.

(LIGHTNING - THUNDER) ―――― *L & T*

VOL. 1

Hope this storm doesn't keep him away.
(Xes up to R. window)

Dick
(warming hands)
He hates driving in the rain.

Tom
(X to L. window)
I don't know that I blame him. That hill down from his house
is really treacherous during a storm.

Dick
(turns to others)
We had a bad scare on it the other day when I was driving
back from the Canajoharie Country Club.

Harry
(Xing to L. of chair L.C.)
How did you get onto that road? We always use the Tallahassee -
Spokane Highway coming from the Club.

Dick
(Xing to cellarette)
Bill Crunch's wife had their car and we were taking him home.
It wouldn't <u>have</u> been . . .

PHONE

(PHONE)

←―――――

Harry
(X to desk R., answers)
Yes?
(listens)
Oh, hello, Molly . . .

John (offstage)― ― ― ― ― ― ― *JOHN*

Miserable night, Jeeves.

Jeeves (off)
It is that, sir.

L & T

VOL. 1

Harry
(hearing voices off)
Just a second, Molly . . .

Note

Pre-set 3 glasses
with ice cubes. Dick
mixes 2 highballs,
puts whiskey in third.

John (off)

Hope it stops soon.

Harry
(into phone)
You don't have to worry, he just arrived.

(JOHN enters) (CARRIES BOOK, WAVES TO OTHERS. Below Desk)

One minute, Molly, and I'll put him on.
(Hands phone to John)
It's Molly, John.
(Xes to C.)

John
(Xes to L. of desk - into phone)
Hello, dear.
(listens)

(DICK joins TOM at cellarette -
both get drinks)

No, no trouble at all. Took it very carefully.
(listens - turns C.)
Now just relax and take it easy - I'll be OK.
(listens - HARRY signals he wants
to talk again)
Certainly, dear, certainly. Harry wants to talk to you again.
(gives Harry phone -
Xes to fireplace)

(Into phone) Harry
Molly, now don't worry. This storm will be over in a halfhour . .

(LIGHTNING - THUNDER) ———— L & T
Vol. 4

at least I think it will be. Everything's under control.
Yes . . . yes . . . Right! Goodbye.
(hangs up - turns C.)

John
(at fireplc)
Molly gets into quite a state on nights like this if I'm out in
it. Spends most of her time on the phone calling the neighbors.
(Harry Xes to radio U.R)

Tom
(Xing U.C.)
Don't blame her. Dick was just telling us he had a bad time
on that hill of yours the other day.
(Harry at radio)

L & T

Harry adds seltzer to
glass - pre-set by Dick

Harry puts down drink
on desk, Xes & shuts
door, returns to desk,
gets drink.

                    Dick
            (X to John)
Fortunately we were just creeping along. Even so we turned
completely around. Nothing else in sight and we stayed on the
road Lucky. Glad I'm walking tonight, aren't you, Tom?

                    Tom   *L & T*
                                           Vol.2
You bet!

                    John
Yes, Molly worries and hangs onto the phone - does all day,
anyway, storm or no storm.

                    Harry
            (Has been at radio U.R. corner, now
             Xes to L.C.)
Nothing but static. Drink, John?
    ⟵   (starts to mix highball)

                    John

Not when I'm driving.

                    Harry

Wise.
            (to others)
Drink? Oh, good, you've already helped yourselves.

                    Tom
            (X & sit chair L.C.)
Can't resist your bourbon, Harry.

            (LIGHTNING - THUNDER)   *L & T*
                                           Vol.1
                    Harry   *WARN*
            (indicating chair U.S. fireplc)   *END*
This suit you, John?   *ACT*

                    John
            (Xing to chair)
My favorite.
            (picks up paper)
How'd the Yankees make out?
            (sits - reads)

Grabbed another.   Harry
~~Won again.~~ Three to one.
            (Xes to desk)
    ⟵

                    Dick
            (Sits chair D.L.)
Poor Red Sox.

Alternate line for Dick
"You mean this getting-things-out-of-
our-systems business?"

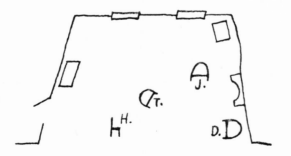

John

(with paper)

Williams got their only run, I see; a homer. I can't understand how such a good team loses so many games.

(pause)

Harry

(pulls desk chair to D.C.)

I've been thinking over what you suggested last week, Tom. I'm
disposed to agree that it might be a good thing for all of us.

Dick

You mean this confession business?

Harry

Yes. You'll remember that Tom thought that it would be beneficial to us all. Need to unload once in a while. Bad for us
to keep anything bottled up too long. I'm all for it. How
about the rest of you?   *(sits)*

Tom

Obviously I'm for it or I would never have suggested it.

Dick

I'll tag along. How about you, John?

John

Well, I . . .

Harry

(quickly, overriding)

Of course John's with us. Tom, as it was your suggestion, how
about you taking the lead?

Tom

Right. I've kept this quiet, as I guess you have the things
you'll tell us. I gamble. Oh, not just a tenth-of-a-cent-
at-bridge sort of thing - I really gamble; dice, roulette,
cards - the works. Fortunately no one at the bank knows it
and fortunately gambling with other people's money doesn't
interest me. Also, I can afford it. But the strain of keeping it under my hat has been terrific. Glad to share it.
*(He Xes to cellarette, gets
more whiskey)*
(Pause)   *L & T*
(JOHN very quiet)   *Vol 3*
Your turn, Dick. *(Tom Xes & sits L.C.)*

Dick

(Blurting it out)

I drink! Of course you've seen me take a drink or two at a
party or like this. I don't mean that. About twice a year

John is getting
more excited —
gleam in eye
$\longrightarrow$

John rubs palms
together
$\longrightarrow$

Dick (con't)
I go up to the cabin with a case or two of whiskey and just
soak it in. I don't shave or bathe - in fact I'm just a sodden
mass - a fine looking surgeon! After about a week I've had
enough and I get straightened out and that's that for another
six months. I hate it but there it is. Now, you too, know.
(Rises, put glass on mantle, sits)
                (Pause)

                        Harry *(takes glass to desk)*
You men have been frank and so shall I. ₓ It's women with me.

                (Astonishment from ALL) └*(sits)*

Yes, you can stare. Harry Hanson, pillar of the church, the
perfect family man with a lovely wife, fine children. I know
what people think and say about me and they might not believe
this but it's true. I, too, periodically go off the track. I
go to the Big City, hide away in a hotel and have women. A
series of them. After it's over I return to my family, whom
I love dearly, and never think of another woman, except my
wife, for many months. And there you have it!

                (another pause)

Well, John, it's up to you.

                (ALL turn to John)

                        John
                (with difficulty)
No. I'm afraid . . . no, I better not.

                        Tom
Come, come. It'll do you good.

                        John
No. It's too terrible. You'd all hate me. You'd never
speak to me again.

                        Harry
You know we all agreed. Certainly you'll tell us. Why,
see how much better we all feel. Come on, now.

                        John
Well, if you really think . . .

                        Dick
It's the best thing.

1-4-44

John
f you'll promise . . .

(The others, simultaneously)

Tom   Dick   Harry
ertainly!   Of course!   Naturally! Naturally!

John
It's like this. I just can't wait 'til morning. I'm a gossip.

(Consternation)

(LIGHTNING - THUNDER)

Vol.4   FAST CURTAIN

1 - FLASH
2 - CURTAIN
3 - WORK LIGHT
4 - PORTAL OUT
5 - TABLE TURN
6 - PORTAL IN
7 - WORK LIGHT OUT
8 - CURTAIN UP

Record #12 between Scenes
on Front Speakers

AT RISE:
        DAISY
        JOHN
    READY:
        MOLLY

DOUBLE-CHECK
Window Shades!!

Stand-by pencils
for Daisy

ACT ONE, Scene 5

WARN
PHONE

(The following morning, John Smithers'
office.)

(AT RISE: DAISY is at her desk, sorting
mail. After a moment JOHN enters.)

                    John
          (Xing to closet, hangs up hat)
Good morning, Miss Caramel.

                    Daisy
          (smiling)
Good morning, Mr. Smithers!

                    John
          (Xing to Daisy's desk)
Got the mail sorted?

          (DAISY hands him several letters)

Good.

          (HE sits at his desk, opens letters.
           DAISY takes notebook and pencil, rises
           Xes to his R. HE reads hurriedly,
           gives letter to Daisy)
Just a short note answering this. The usual "Sorry, conditions
do not warrant further expansion at this time."

          (DAISY takes letter, makes note.
           JOHN picks up another letter)
Well, well. Good thing we never finished that letter yesterday,
Miss Caramel. Here's one from ... ha, ha ... "supalia" ... ha, ha!

                    Daisy

Oh, how fortunate.   *PHONE*

          (PHONE)

          (DAISY Xes to her desk, puts notebook,
           pencil, letter on desk, sits facing
           front)

                    Daisy (con't)
          (into phone)
John Smithers' office, Miss Caramel speaking.
          (listens)
          (JOHN is busy with letter)
He's right here, Miss Lammerton.

John must have 10 letters) ⟶

COSTUMES!!

Get Molly's change-room ready

(JOHN looks up. DAISY listens, turns
to John, pantomimes "no", JOHN turns
back to letter)

                    Daisy (con't)
Certainly. I'll tell him.
                    (hangs up)
                    (to John)
That was Miss Lammerton, Dr. Richard Bestor's office nurse.
Dr. Bestor won't be able to have lunch with you today. He
left town suddenly and won't be back for two weeks.

                    John
                    (looking up)
Oh?

                    Daisy
He went to his camp.
                    (turns back to work)

                    John
                    (with speculative gleam)
Ohhh?

                    (JOHN is lost in thought. His look
                    settles on Daisy - new idea comes)

Miss Caramel . . .

                    Daisy
                    (half turns head)
Yes, Mr. Smithers?

                    John
Miss Caramel, has Mr. Harry Hanson ever

            etc.   etc.

ACT ONE, Scene 4

Decanter, 4 glasses, soda siphon

Phone

Newspaper

Door OPEN

Shades UP

Fireplace FLICKER

Rain

ACT ONE, Scene 5

Letters on Daisy's desk

etc.

etc.

PROPERTIES

ACT ONE, Scene 4

ON STAGE

      Table-desk, stg R.
          Blotter, inkstand, phone, calendar
      Straight chair by desk
      Console radio, magazine on top
      Green brocade drapes on windows
      Roller shades on windows
      Book cases and books (not practical)
      Cellarette
          Whiskey, 4 glasses, ice, siphon (all practical)
      2 comfortable armchairs
      1 armchair - smaller
      Evening Newspaper

OFFSTAGE & HAND

      Book off D.R. (JOHN)

ACT ONE, Scene 5

      etc.   etc.

LIGHT CUES

Act One, Scene 3 (cont)

Number	Cue	Description	Mark
14	"Curtain"	Front Lights **OUT**	OUT
	SET SCENE 4		
15	"Start Rain"	Rain effect	Full
16	"Curtain Up"	Front Lights UP	7
17 18 19 20 21 22 23 24 25	On word "Flash" from Stage Manager	Lightning Special (quick flash)	Full
26	"Curtain"	Front Lights OUT	Out
	SET SCENE 5		
27	"Curtain Up"	Front Lights Up	Full
	etc.	etc.	

SOUND CUES

ACT ONE, Scene 3 (cont)

Num-ber	Cue	Description	Rec-ord	Origin	Volume	Speaker
#9	From Stg. Mgr.	Hanson's Voice	#10	Table 1	30	Phone on stage
10	"	"	"	"	Count 6 to out	"
11	"Work Lights"	Filibuster's Voice	11	Table 2	40	Fronts
12	"Work Lights"	"	"	"	Fast Out	"
		Scene 4				
13	"Curtain Up"Watch Flash - Count 3	Thunder	XXX	Screen Vol 4	60	Bk Stg
14	Flash Count 3	"	XXX	Vol 1	"	"
15	Flash Count 1	"	XXX	Vol 4	"	"
16	Flash Count 3	"	XXX	Vol 1	"	"
17	Flash Count 1	"	XXX	Vol 4	"	"
18	Flash Count 2	"	XXX	Vol 2	"	"
19	Flash Count 4	"	XXX	Vol 1	"	"
20	Flash Count 3	"	XXX	Vol 3	"	"
21	Flash,Instantanus No Count	"	XXX	Vol 20	80	Bk stg & Front
22	"Work Lights	Thunder,street noise,typing	12	Table 1	40	Fronts
23	"Work Light Out"	"	"	"	Fast Out	"
		Scene 5				
	etc.	etc.			etc.	

(Notes to the reader concerning Appendix B)

1. The stage manager uses an intercom system and delivers cues orally.

2. The numbered cues at the end of each scene are the exact words spoken. In small productions the stage manager may not find it necessary to tabulate his orders. However, in this production, it was felt necessary to do so, because the exact order of execution is vital. E.g., the portal must be out of the way before the revolving stage turns, and the stage must stop turning before the portal is returned into place. The stage manager was taking no chances.

   Sometimes an individual order means different things to different personnel, E.g., end of Scene 4, Cue #2, "CURTAIN,"

   Means: Curtain Down—to curtain men
   Front Lights Out—to electrician
   Stop Rain—to rain operator

3. The stage manager handles phone bells personally, and so they do not appear on Sound Cue Sheet.

4. The sound operator takes the actual lightning flash as his cue for thunder. An amplified screen is used for thunder. The volumes indicate the strength with which the screen is struck..

C. The Finished Prompt Script

                          John
Whenever I find that the . . .

                    (TELEPHONE RINGS)

                          Daisy
                  (picks up phone from her desk)
John Smithers' office, Miss Caramel speaking.

                    (HANSON'S voice is heard over the phone.
                    No words are discernible, but the tone
                    of his voice is angry and excited.
                    DAISY holds receiver away from ear when
                    he speaks and each time HANSON pauses
                    DAISY tries to speak.)

Yes, Mr. Han . . .

                    (HANSON again)

But, if you'd just let me . . .

                    (HANSON again)

                    (JOHN , quietly amused, picks up his
                    extension from his desk and takes charge.)

                          John
Listen, you old bag of wind, settle down!

                    (DAISY replaces her phone - starts
                    writing in her notebook.)

                    (HANSON continues angrily - after a
                    moment, quiets down.)

                    (JOHN rises, walks upstage to limit of
                    phone receiver wire, comesback, picks
                    up phone base, walks dnstage to limit
                    of wire, Xes back to his desk, listens.)

                          John (con't)
Fine! Fine! I'll see you tonight about eight-thirty.
                    (HE replaces phone, Xes to L. of Daisy.)
Hanson can drown out a brass band when he gets started. Hard on the
ears . . .
                    (slyly)
especially such pretty pink ones, like yours.

                          Daisy
                    (embarrassed, looks at desk)
Oh, Mister Smithers!

John
(resuming office manner, Xes to his chair)
Yes, yes, ah . . . well, yes. I think we have time for one more letter.
(HE sits)

Daisy
(with no expression)
Certainly, Mr. Smithers.
(takes notebook from drawer, picks up
pencil, turns to John.)

John
(dictating)
"Mr. A. Brush Wallaby"
(aside to Daisy, small smile)
Put this on my personal stationery. You'll find his address in my
personal address book under Australia.
(dictating)
"Dear Wally" comma "Long time no hear from" dash "what goes" question
mark. "Anxious to hear how things progress with all the supalia"
period. That's . . .
(spelling)
. . . s - u - p - a - l - i - a . . .
(explaining, self-consciously)
you know, plural diminutive of marsupial. Ha, ha! Well, ahem, ah . . .
(resumes dictation)
"Molly and the kids pester the life out of me asking me when . . .

(TELELPHONE RINGS)

(DAISY turns front, puts down notebook,
answers phone.)

Daisy
(into phone)
John Smithers' office, Miss Caramel speaking.
(listens a moment)
Why, yes, Mr. Filibuster.

(JOHN startled rises, Xes D.C., turns to
Daisy, gestures wildly that he is "not in"
has "gone out". DAISY pretends not to
understand, continues to listen to phone.
JOHN re-enacts "not in" business. SHE
nods she understands. JOHN smiles, gets
hat from closet, starts out, pats Daisy's
shoulder, exits. DAISY alone, straightens

things on her desk, as she continues
to listen to Filibuster.)

                CURTAIN - MEDIUM SLOW

(During the scene change there are no house
lights but over the loud speakers in the
auditorium Filibuster's voice may be heard.
Most of what he says is a confused jumble of
words with occasional clear passages. Daisy's
voice comes through weakly at intervals,"Yes,
Mr. Filibuster" and "No, Mr. Filibuster"
being the extent of what she says. The sound
dies away just as the curtain rises on Scene 4.)

ACT ONE, Scene 4

(The curtain has just left the floor when
there is a terrific clap of thunder.
After it rises Harry Hanson's workroom
is revealed. It is shortly after eight,
the same evening. It is raining.)

(The room is small and comfortable with
well-worn chairs, and shelves for many
books. D.R. an open door to hall. In
U.R. corner a console radio. Above door
against R. wall a table-desk with straight
chair. Built-in bookcase in R. wall. Two
windows upstage with bookcase between.
Curtains not drawn. In U.L. corner a
cellarette with glasses, decanter, soda,
ice ready. Fireplace with fire burning
in C. of L. wall. Above fireplace facing
D.S., easy chair. D.L. against wall
facing Stg R., easy chair. C. windsor
chair facing fireplace.)

(AT RISE: HARRY, in gray slacks and smoking
jacket, sits in chair U.S. of fireplace,
reading newspaper.)

                    Tom (offstage)
What a storm!

          (HARRY looks up)
          (LIGHTNING & THUNDER)

                    Jeeves (off)
Very wet, sir. Yes, sir.

                    Dick (off)
Better put those coats in the kitchen, Jeeves.

          (HARRY puts paper in chair, rises, Xes C.)

                    Jeeves (off)
Yes, sir.

          (TOM ALBION and DICK BESTOR enter thru door)

          (Tom Albion is a man of 35, tall and dark.
          He wears a tweed suit. Dick Bestor, about 45,
          is short and stocky with iron-gray hair,
          wears a dark blue business suit.)

                              Harry
Glad you could make it tonight, Tom.

                    (THEY shake hands)

                              Tom
You know I never miss these sessions, Harry.
                    (Xes U.L.)

                              Harry
                    (with mock formality)
Richard Bestor! Doctor Richard Bestor!
                    (then, easily)
How are you, Dick, you old sawbones?

                              Dick

Fine, Harry, just fine!

                    (THEY shake hands. DICK Xes to fireplace)

                              Harry
                    (still C.)
Make yourselves comfortable. John should be along any minute now. I
talked to him on the phone this afternoon - said he'd try to get here by
eight-thirty.

                    (LIGHTNING & THUNDER)

Hope this storm doesn't keep him away.
                    (Xes up to R. window)

                              Dick
                    (warming hands, back to room)
He hates driving in the rain.

                              Tom
                    (X to L. window)
I don't know that I blame him. That hill down from his house is really
treacherous during a storm.

                              Dick
                    (turns to others)
We had a bad scare on it the other day when I was driving back from the
Canajoharie Country Club.

                              Harry
                    (Xing to L. of chair L.C.)
How did you get onto that road? We always use the Tallahassee-Spokane
Highway coming from the Club.

                    Dick
              (Xing to cellarette)
Bill Crunch's wife had their car and we were taking him home. It
wouldn't have been . . .

                 (TELEPHONE RINGS)

                    Harry
              (Xes to desk R., answers)
Yes?
              (listens)
Oh, hello, Molly . . .

                         John (offstage)
Miserable night, Jeeves.

                 (LIGHTNING & THUNDER)

                         Jeeves (off)
It is that, sir.

                    Harry
              (hearing voices off)
Just a second, Molly . . .

                         John (off)
Hope it stops soon.

                    Harry
              (into phone)
You don't have to worry, he just arrived.

                    (JOHN enters wearing same suit as in
                    Scene 3. He carries a book. HE
                    waves "hello" to others. Xes to
                    below desk.)

One minute, Molly, and I'll put him on.
                    (hands phone to John)
It's Molly, John.
                    (HARRY Xes to C.)

                         John
                    (Xes to L. of desk, puts down book)
                    (Into phone)
Hello, dear.

                    (listens)

                    (TOM joins DICK at cellarette - both
                    get drinks)

John (con't)
No, no trouble at all. Took it very carefully.
(listens - turns C.)
Now just relax and take it easy - I'll be OK.
(listens. HARRY signals he wants to
talk to her again.)
Certainly, dear, certainly. Harry wants to talk to you again.
(gives HARRY phone - Xes to fireplace)

Harry
(into phone)
Molly, now don't you worry. This storm will be over in a halfhour . . .

(LIGHTNING & THUNDER)

at least I think it will be. Everything's under control. Yes . . .
yes . . . Right! Goodbye.
(hangs up - turns C.)

John
(back to fire)
Molly gets into quite a state on nights like this if I'm out in it.
Spends most of her time on the phone calling the neighbors.

(HARRY Xes to radio U.R.)

Tom
(Xing U.C. with highball)
Don't blame her. Dick was just telling us he had a bad time on that hill
of yours the other day.

(HARRY fiddles with radio)

Dick
(X to John - has highball)
Fortunately we were just creeping along. Even so we turned completely
around. Nothing else in sight, and we stayed on the road. Lucky. Glad
I'm walking tonight, aren't you, Tom?

(LIGHTNING & THUNDER)

Tom

You bet!

John
Yes, Molly worries and hangs onto the phone - does it all day, anyway,
storm or no storm. Ha, ha!

                         Harry
                (Has been at radio U.R. corner, now
                Xes to U.L.)
Nothing but static. Drink, John?
                (starts to mix highball)

                         John

Not when I'm driving.

                         Harry
Wise.
                (to others)
Drink? Oh, good, you've already helped yourselves.

                         Tom
                (X & sit chair L.C.)
Can't resist your bourbon, Harry.

                (LIGHTNING & THUNDER)

                         Harry
                (indicating chair U.S. fireplace)
This suit you, John?

                         John
                (Xing to chair)
My favorite.
                (picks up newspaper)
How'd the Yankees make out?
                (sits - reads)

                         Harry
                (Xes to desk - puts down drink)
Grabbed another. Three to one.

                         Dick
                (sits chair D.L.)
Poor Red Sox.

                (HARRY Xes to door, closes it. Xes
                back to desk, picks up drink.)

                         John
                (with newspaper)
Williams got their only run, I see; a homer. I can't understand how
such a good team loses so many games.

                (Pause - each with own thoughts)

                         Harry
                (Pulls desk chair to D.C.)
I've been thinking over what you suggested last week, Tom. I'm disposed
to agree that it might be a good thing for all of us.

                              Dick
You mean this getting-things-out-of-our-system business?

                             Harry
Yes. You'll remember that Tom thought that it would be beneficial to us
all. Need to unload once in a while. Bad for us to keep anything bottled
up too long. I'm all for it.
                    (sits)
How about the rest of you?

                              Tom
Obviously I'm for it or I would never have suggested it.

                             Dick
I'll tag along. How about you, John?

                             John

Well, I . . .

                             Harry
                  (quickly - overriding)
Of course John's with us. Tom, as it was your suggestion, how about
you taking the lead?

                    (THEY have formed a group-of-three downstage
                    of John and only occasionally throw him a
                    glance. JOHN, unnoticed, grows more and
                    more excited as the others tell their stories.
                    When each finishes and there is general move-
                    ment and looking around, JOHN freezes.)

                              Tom
Right. I've kept this quiet, as I guess you have the things you'll tell
us. I gamble. Oh, not just a tenth-of-a-cent-at-bridge sort of thing -
I really gamble; dice, roulette, cards - the works. Fortunately no one
at the bank knows it and fortunately gambling with other people's money
doesn't interest me. Also, I can afford it. But the strain of keeping
it under my hat has been terrific. Glad to share it.

                    (LIGHTNING & THUNDER)

                    (TOM Xes to cellarette, gets more whiskey)

                    (A pause - JOHN is very quiet)

                         Tom (con't)
Your turn, Dick.
                    (Xes and sits L.C.)

                             Dick
                    (Blurting it out)
I drink! Of course you've seen me take a drink or two at a party or like

                              Dick (con't)
this. I don't mean that. About twice a year I go up to the cabin with
a case or two of whiskey and just soak it in. I don't shave or bathe -
in fact I'm just a sodden mass - a fine looking surgeon! After about a
week I've had enough and I get straightened out and that's that for another
six months. I hate it but there it is. Now you, too, know.
                    (HE rises, puts glass on mantel,
                     sits again.)

                    (A pause - JOHN has gleam in eye)

                              Harry
                    (who has gone to desk, leaves glass,
                     returns)
You men have been frank and so shall I.
                    (sits)
It's women with me.

                    (Astonishment from ALL -
                     JOHN rubs palms together)

Yes, you can stare. Harry Hanson, pillar of the church, the perfect
family man with a lovely wife, fine children. I know what people think
and say about me and they might not believe this but it's true. I, too,
periodically go off the track. I go to the Big City, hide away in a
hotel and have women. A series of them. After it's over I return to my
family, whom I love dearly, and never think of another woman, except my
wife, for many months. And there you have it!

                    (Another pause)

Well, John, it's up to you.

                    (ALL turn to John)

                              John
                    (with difficulty)
No. I'm afraid . . . no, I better not.

                              Tom
Come, come. It'll do you good.

                              John
No. It's too terrible. You'd all hate me. You'd never speak to me
again.

                              Harry
You know we all agreed. Certainly you'll tell us. Why, see how much
better we all feel. Come on, now.

John

Well, if you really think . . .

Dick

It's the best thing.

John

If you'll promise . . .

(ALL - simultaneously)

Tom	Dick	Harry
Certainly!	Of course!	Naturally! Naturally!

John

It's like this. I just can't wait 'til morning. I'm a gossip!

(Consternation)

(LIGHTNING & THUNDER, FORTISSIMO)

FAST   CURTAIN

(Between the scenes there are no house lights.
The sound of thunder rolls about the auditorium
coming from the loud speakers. The thunder soon
blends into the roar of city traffic. The traffic
noises become more and more staccato and are dis-
placed by the clackety-clack of a typewriter. The
typing noise fades away as the curtain rises on
Scene 5.)

ACT ONE, Scene 5

(John Smithers' office, the following
morning. It is as we last saw it except
that it looks "cleaned" and "arranged".
Letters that were scattered are now in
neat piles, chairs are squared up along
side of the desks, the window shades are
even, wastebaskets are empty, etc.

(AT RISE: DAISY is sitting at her desk,
sorting mail. SHE has just finished
when JOHN enters from R.)

                    John
          (Xing to closet, hangs up hat)
Good morning, Miss Caramel.

                    Daisy
          (smiling)
Good morning, Mr. Smithers..

          etc.   etc.

PROPERTY PLOT

Act One, Scene 4

Stage Right Wall (D.S.R. to Up)
    Over door, mounted fish (small)
    Desk C. of wall
            On top of desk:
                    Desk set
                    Phone
                    Student lamp (practical, see LIGHTS)
    Over desk, on wall
            Framed antique map, no glass
    Up stage of desk - built-in book shelves
            Books - not practical
    In U.R. corner - Console radio (not practical)
            6 magazines on top

Back wall (R. to L.)
    R.C. of wall - window
            Heavy green velour drapes with valance
            Dark green roller shade - halfway down
    C. of wall - built-in book shelves
            Books - not practical
    L.C. of wall - window
            Ditto other window

Stage Left Wall (Up stage L. to Down)
    In U.L. corner - Cellarette
            On top, ready to use - all practical
                    Silver tray holding: glass ice bucket with cube
                            ice, silver ice tongs, decanter of whiskey,
                            stopper, 4 highball glasses, siphon of
                            soda (Sparklet)
                    Small lamp (practical - see LIGHTS)
    On wall above cellarette - small hunting print
    C. of wall - fireplace
            On mantel - 2 small loving cups, small model sailing
                            ship
    On wall above fireplace - mounted sailfish
    Down stg fireplace, against wall - large green overstuffed chair
    On wall over chair - hunting print
    Down stg of chair - floor lamp - practical (see LIGHTS)

Up stage of fireplace, facing front, large brown overstuffed chair
    Newspaper in seat
L.C. facing fireplace - mahogany windsor chair
L. of desk - mahogany straight chair

Carpet - wall to wall neutral green

Offstage D.R.
    Book, The Houses In Between   (JOHN)

LIGHT PLOT

Note to reader: At the beginning of the light plot there is a list of all equipment, including each instrument and its number, where it is placed, its color gelatine, its focus, and the area it lights. And so for each scene it is not necessary to repeat this information—only the instrument number, intensity, and change need be noted.

LIGHT PLOT

ACT ONE, Scene 4

FRONT LIGHTS:
      #3, 4, 5, 6, 7, 8, 9, 10, all 3/4 up

1st PIPE: #4 -- Full
          5 -- Full
          6 -- 1/2 up
          7 -- Full
       10 -- 3/4 up
       11 -- Full
       13 -- 1/2 up
       14 -- Full
       15 -- Full
    X-rays -- Amber only - 1/4 up

OVER DOOR R. (off):
      4-compartment strip, 25 watt, frosted light amber

DESK STAGE R.:
      Student lamp - practical

CELLARETTE U.L. CORNER:
      Small lamp, parchment shade - practical

DOWN STAGE L.:
      Floor lamp, parchment shade - practical

RAIN EFFECT:
      Outside windows Up stge - thruout scene

FIREPLACE FLICKER:
      Thruout scene

LIGHTNING FLASH
      Outside windows - thruout scene on cue

NO FOOTS

NO CHANGE OF LIGHT ON STAGE

Note to reader: Here is added a copy of "Light Cues"—the same as in Appendix B.

SOUND PLOT

Note to reader: As in the light plot, the sound plot starts with a list of equipment, including descriptions of all records and effects. Thus the plot for each scene will be a listing of cues, as illustrated in Appendix B.

COSTUME PLOT

COSTUME PLOT

Act One, Scene 4

HARRY:
       Maroon, solid-colored smoking jacket
       Dark gray flannel slacks
       White negligee shirt - no tie
       Plain brown socks
       Dark brown loafers

TOM:
       Brown tweed suit
       White shirt, button down collar - bow tie
       Argyle socks
       Dark brown oxfords

DICK:
       Dark blue worsted suit
       Light blue shirt - white line
       Black and crimson striped four-in-hand
       Dark socks
       Black oxfords

JOHN:
       (Same as Act One, Scene 3)

SCENERY PLOT

Note to reader: This will be a brief, informative description of how the scenery is handled. In this case mention of the revolving stage (turntable), of which backings are flown or run, of any specialties such as quick-change rooms, together with small-scale drawings of the ground plans and full-stage photos of the settings should suffice.

ACT ONE, Sc. 4

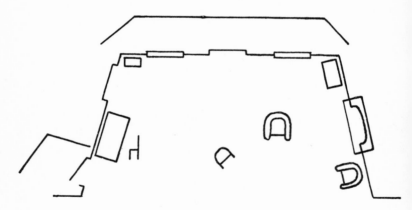

1/8" = 1'

D. Selected Union Rules

Any attempt to list all the rules of the various theatrical unions would be almost certainly doomed to failure. Such a list would be obsolete before it could reach publication, because union rules undergo constant change and revision.

Only those rules, and also traditions, which concern the stage manager in his work have been included. The reader may use this list as a guide, but should not consider it exhaustive or authoritative for all circumstances and for all time.

ACTORS' EQUITY RULES AND TRADITIONS

Contracts

1. The stage manager does not work, even before rehearsals, without a contract stipulating his salary. Consequently, a stage manager always works for full pay.

2. Stage managers do not act parts.

3. Stage managers are not regular understudies, but may substitute in extreme emergencies.

4. Assistant stage managers must have contracts, and work for full salary at all times.

5. Assistant stage managers may act parts and/or understudy.

6. Actors may not rehearse without a contract.

Rehearsals

1. Notify Equity of the date, time, and place of the first rehearsal.

2. Prepare a list of all actors, understudies, and stage man-

agers. A representative from Equity will collect this list at the first rehearsal.

3. Receive from the Equity representative a Deputy Selection Sheet.

4. Immediately after the five-day probationary period is over, and actors are "set," have the company select an Equity Deputy. The Deputy must be a Senior Member in good standing.

5. Rehearsal pay for all actors is forty dollars a week, except for stage managers, who receive full salary. Rehearsal pay is for a full, seven-day week.

6. First day of rehearsal is the day on which any actor is first called to attend a rehearsal. A reading of the play, as a preliminary to walking rehearsals, is considered a rehearsal. All actors are not necessarily called the same day. Thus the first rehearsal day for each actor need not be the same. Either a reading by the actors or a reading to the actors (by the director or anyone else) is considered a reading of the play.

(There is another form of "reading the play." This is a formal reading to enable the producer to evaluate a manuscript. Actors are hired at a nominal, but Equity-established and -controlled, salary for this one reading and one purpose. This is not the type of reading referred to when "reading the play" is used in conjunction with regular rehearsals of the play.)

7. An actor who is called for a rehearsal, and who appears at rehearsal, even though he may not rehearse, or may be dismissed immediately, is considered to have rehearsed that day.

8. The probationary period for each actor is the first five days of his rehearsal. During that period, and before the company is dismissed on the fifth day of his rehearsal, the actor may be discharged without formality other than that he be told of his discharge, in writing, by the producer or his representative.

The actor need not actually rehearse during these five days. If the actor has been legally called to rehearsal, has attended rehearsals, or has been dismissed from rehearsal because he is not to be rehearsed, and has not been formally and legally discharged from his job, he has fulfilled the requirements of the probationary period and, after the end of rehearsals on his fifth day, his contract is legal and binding.

9. Nonmusical plays are allowed four rehearsal weeks immediately preceding the first public performance. The actor receives full salary after four rehearsal weeks, whether or not public performances are given.

EXCEPT: If an out-of-town tryout tour is made, any unused rehearsal days may be utilized immediately before the New York opening.

This schedule may clarify this point:

1st week—	Rehearsals	—Rehearsal Salary
2nd week—	Rehearsals	—Rehearsal Salary
3rd week—	Rehearsals	—Rehearsal Salary
4th week—{	3 days, Dress Rehearsals	—Rehearsal Salary
	3 days, out-of-town tryout	—Full Salary
5th week—	Out-of-town tryout performances	—Full Salary
6th week—	Out-of-town tryout performances	—Full Salary
7th week—{	4 days of rehearsal in N.Y.C. (the days not used in 4th week). These days may include dress rehearsals.	—Rehearsal Salary
	Any additional rehearsal days, previews of any type, the N.Y. opening, and thereafter	—Full Salary

10. Rehearsal Hours:

a) There are no limitations placed on the stage managers' working hours. That is one of the reasons they receive full salary.

b) The rehearsal week is seven days, including Sundays and holidays. It may start on any day of the week. Sundays or other days, if not used for rehearsals, are "lost" days, and additional days may not be added at the end of the rehearsal weeks to compensate.

c) During the first three weeks of rehearsal, actors' rehearsals are limited to eight consecutive hours. Of these eight hours, one must be allotted as a meal (or rest) hour.

Sample legal schedule for all actors during first three weeks:

> 10 A.M.   to 12 Noon—Rehearsal
> 12 Noon to 1 P.M.   —Meal Hour
> 1 P.M.   to 6 P.M.   —Rehearsal

These are eight consecutive hours with one hour out for a meal.

Illegal schedule for all actors:

> 10 A.M. to 1 P.M.—Rehearsal
> 1 P.M. to 4 P.M.—Meal (or Rest) Hour
> 4 P.M. to 8 P.M.—Rehearsal

Although only seven hours are used for rehearsal, they do not fall within the eight-consecutive-hour limit.

Legal schedule if groups, or shifts, of actors are used:

> 10 A.M.   to 12 Noon—Rehearsal for Group A
> 12 Noon to 1 P.M. —Meal Hour
> 1 P.M.   to 6 P.M. —Rehearsal for Groups A & B
> 6 P.M.   to 7 P.M. —Meal Hour. Group A dismissed
> 7 P.M.   to 9 P.M. —Rehearsal for Groups B & C
>   9 P.M. —Dismiss Group B
> 9 P.M.   to 2 A.M. —Rehearse Group C, if desired

No group of actors has rehearsed more than eight consecutive hours, and each group has had one hour for a meal. The stage managers have worked all three shifts.

d) Appointments for costume fittings, publicity, and the like may be scheduled for before or after rehearsals. However, as the working hours for most establishments coincide with re-hearsal hours, it is customary to arrange appointments for times when the actor is not required at rehearsals, or vice versa.

e) Special performances or rehearsals for recordings are part of the eight-hour rehearsal period. Other special rehearsals, such as fencing or dancing lessons, are also a part of the eight-hour period. However, an actor who is hired because he is supposedly proficient in a specialty, and then finds he needs tutoring, will arrange for such tutoring at his own expense, and outside the eight-hour rehearsal period.

f) Beginning six days before the first paid public performance, the eight-hour-rehearsal-day rule is no longer operative. During these six days, rehearsals may be held at all hours, provided a maximum of twelve consecutive hours is not exceeded. However, out of each twenty-four hours, ten hours' consecutive rest must be given the actor. During these ten hours, no rehearsals, costume fittings, etc. may be held. During the remaining work hours, proper rest periods and meal hours must be furnished. Also two work periods may not be joined together.

THIS SCHEDULE IS ILLEGAL:

1st 24 hrs.—
- 10 A.M. to 10 P.M.—Rehearsals, with proper rest periods
- 10 P.M. to 8 A.M.—Uninterrupted free time for actors

2nd 24 hrs.—
- 8 A.M. to 6 P.M.—Free time for actors
- 6 P.M. to 2 A.M.—Rehearsal Period A

3rd 24 hrs.— 10 A.M. to 10 P.M.—Rehearsal Period B

In the above schedule, the last rehearsal period (Period B) is illegal. The fact that a ten-hour period preceded Rehearsal Period A does not alter the situation. From 6 P.M. in the second twenty-four hours to 6 P.M. in the third twenty-four hours constitutes, in itself, a twenty-four-hour period. There were sixteen hours of rehearsal in *that* twenty-four hours. If

Rehearsal Period B had started at twelve Noon, then the schedule would have been legal.

g) During the tryout tour, after the final rehearsal week and after the out-of-town opening, the workday reverts to the eight-hour schedule. The performance, computed at three hours by Actors' Equity, is part of the workday. Thus five hours are available for rehearsal on most days, and two hours on matinee days.

The ten-hour rest period between workdays must be maintained for the actors. Train trips are sometimes part of the workday, and sometimes part of the rest hours.

EXAMPLE 1. A daylight Sunday move from Boston to Washington takes nine hours. No rehearsal should be called that Sunday.

EXAMPLE 2. A trip from Boston to Philadelphia takes about six hours. However, the actual train used will determine whether or not a rehearsal should be called on arrival in Philadelphia. If the actors take an 8 A.M. train Sunday morning, they have not had ten hours' rest following Saturday night's performance. No rehearsal should be called that day. On the other hand, if an 11 A.M. train is taken, actors will have had over ten hours' rest. Arrival in Philadelphia will be about 5 P.M. A short evening rehearsal is permissible.

EXAMPLE 3. A train leaving Boston at midnight Saturday arrives in Philadelphia around 7:30 A.M. Actors moved on this train would occupy sleepers and the time consumed is considered part of the rest hours. A rehearsal call in Philadelphia Sunday afternoon would be proper.

NOTE: Actors' Equity is cognizant of the fact that traveling conditions for touring companies are becoming increasingly difficult, that tryout tours are harassed by emergencies, and consequently appreciates that all touring actors must be prepared for a certain amount of give and take. Nevertheless, the above examples indicate the general attitude Equity has toward the welfare of its members.

h) Rehearsal days in New York City, after the tryout tour

and immediately preceding the New York opening, that utilize unused rehearsal days left over from before the tour have their hours limited according to the rehearsal period from which they come. If they are unused days from the first-three-weeks period, the eight-hour rule is effective. If they are from the last-week or "unlimited rehearsal" period, the twelve-hour rule is effective.

i) The stage managers are on call twenty-four hours a day at all times.

Rehearsals after N.Y. Opening. Sufficient company and/or understudy rehearsals are permitted after the New York opening to maintain a high standard of performance. The eight-hour workday, performances included, is effective.

Equity Deputy. The Equity Deputy is an actor in the company of the play he represents. He is the spokesman and official union representative for all Actors' Equity members in his company, including the stage managers. There must be a Deputy for each company of a play, in New York City or on tour. The Deputy must be a Senior Member of Equity, and he must be in good standing. The stage manager is not eligible for the position of Deputy.

The Deputy has jurisdiction over such matters as rehearsal and performance hours and conditions, arranging benefit performances, and collecting dues. He does not have jurisdiction over production matters, or over the running of the performance, except in cases of violation of Equity regulations. In other words, he is a union liaison, not a production staff member.

The Deputy has the use of the call board for posting official Equity notices. Generally a portion of the call board is reserved for his use.

STAGE HANDS UNION RULES

(Wardrobe women are included in these rules, although not always mentioned specifically. Their duties, etc., are approximately parallel to those of the other production crew heads.)

Early Rehearsal Period.   Practically all theaters in New York City that are used for rehearsals are under the jurisdiction of the Stage Hands Union. However, no stage hand need be hired for a rehearsal, if these rules are followed:

1. LIGHTS.   Only the permanent stage work lights may be used. Or, if a production is in residence, the work lights for that production. A maximum of 1000 watts of white light is permitted.

2. SCENERY.   No scenery of any type may be used. Or, if the stage has a permanent setting, no variation to it may be made.

3. PROPERTIES.   Only substitute rehearsal properties may be used.

4. COSTUMES.   Substitute accessories (shoes, handkerchiefs, hats, fans, pin-on trains, etc.) may be used.

5. SOUND.   Substitute makeshifts may be used, e.g., a bicycle bell for a phone bell, a slapstick for a gunshot, etc.

If more elaborate facilities are required, stage hands in the proper department must be hired.

There are a few theaters (in schools, hotels, and office buildings) and many rehearsal halls (hotel ballrooms, clubrooms, etc.) that are not under the jurisdiction of the Stage Hands Union. Anything may be used in these rehearsal places. However, their inaccessibility and limited space practically eliminates utilizing elaborate rehearsal accouterments.

The rule for marking ground plans on the stage floors of theaters under the jurisdiction of the Stage Hands Union is simple. *Only a stage hand may make such markings.* If the markings are to be made permanently on the stage floor, or temporarily on a ground cloth, using paint (oil or water color), chalk, tapes, or any other method that may be devised, the theater's three house crew heads are hired to make the markings. They are hired for a three-hour minimum call. If a temporary ground cloth, marked or unmarked, is used especially for rehearsals, stage hands handle it. If ground cloths are laid before rehearsals and removed after, or transferred to another place of rehearsal, stage hands handle them.

The stage manager does not apply ground plan markings. He may make a very few temporary chalk marks to indicate doors, stairs, etc., but he must not stretch the markings into elaborate plans.

Manufacture and Handling of the Physical Production. The manufacture of the elements of the production is done in union shops under the supervision of the designer or designers. The selection of ready-made articles may be made by anyone.

The transfer of the physical elements from shops to the theater, or from baggage cars or storage houses to the theater, is handled by the Theatrical Transfer Union. Delivery is made to the door of the theater. There the elements are received by the stage hands, and the Transfer Union's jurisdiction ends.

Once in the theater, all elements are handled, assembled, operated, and maintained by stage hands only. There is one exception for all productions—painting, repainting, or retouching of scenery is done by a member of the United Scenic Artists Local, who is known as a scenic artist or retouch man. There will be other exceptions for some productions, usually in matters of installation of special elements at the first setup. These would include special structural steelwork, elaborate draperies, complicated carpeting, linoleum laying, and such things. They are installed by a specialist, usually not a stage hand. However, once installed, they are operated and maintained by stage hands.

In the theater the elements are divided into categories or departments and are handled by members of the proper department and not by members of other departments.

EXAMPLE:

An operator (electrician) is hired to move a lighting instrument during a scenery change. This is his one and only duty. He may be utilized for other work in the Electrical Department, if such work can be found. He may not be borrowed by the Property or Carpentry Departments, even though he may be idle. If the Property or Carpentry Departments need more help, they hire more clearers and grips. The operator remains an operator and is not permitted in the other departments.

Actors and stage managers do not handle, operate, or maintain the physical elements of the production, except as required by the stage action of the play. This does not mean that actors and stage managers are forbidden to touch things. It means this: actors and stage managers must not handle an element for the purpose, conscious or unconscious, of eliminating the services of a stage hand. This general rule applies: stage hands move and operate the elements, actors and stage managers may adjust them.

EXAMPLE:

A desk, with its accessories, is carried onto the stage and set on its markings by stage hands only. The accessories on top of, or in, the desk may be rearranged or adjusted by an actor or stage manager, without the help or attendance of a stage hand.

EXAMPLE:

Stage managers will operate the controls of intercom systems, and of cuing systems. They will not install or maintain such systems. They will operate phone bells and other self-contained sound effects. They will not operate elaborate electronic sound equipment, unless a stage hand, otherwise unoccupied, stands by.

Costumes are handled and maintained by wardrobe women. While touring, the costumes are packed by the wardrobe women, but the loaded trunks, hampers, boxes, etc. are handled by the Property Department.

Classification of Stage Hands.   Stage hands may be divided into three general groups:

1. HOUSE CREW HEADS.   The heads of the three departments (Carpenter, Property, Electrical) are hired by the theater on a seasonal contract. They receive a weekly salary for the weeks a production is in residence. In New York City they must be members of Theatrical Protective Union Local #1, IATSE. There is no house wardrobe woman.

2. PRODUCTION CREW. These are specialists, hired by the producer, who are part of the producer's staff. There may be one or more for each department, or there may be none. They are hired by contract and receive a weekly salary. Their contract is different from the house crew heads', and is known as a "road contract." Their employment is for a specific job—tryout tour, New York run, regular tour, or all three. They may be members of any IA Local in the United States or Canada.

3. CASUALS. Individual members of Local #1 (or of the local in the city where the production is playing), hired for a specific job. These jobs include loading and unloading baggage cars; taking in, setting up, taking down, putting out, or working the performance of a production; and any incidental repair or rehearsal work required. (The title used by members of the IA for these individuals is "stage hand." However, as "stage hand" is also the generic title for all members of the Stage Hands Union, "casual" is used to differentiate these individuals from house heads and production crew. These casuals may also be identified by the department to which they are assigned—car loader, grip, clearer or handler, and operator.)

Working Hours. PRODUCTION CREW. These men are hired on a twenty-four-hour-a-day, seven-day-a-week basis. They receive a flat salary, and get no overtime.

HOUSE CREW HEADS. The house crew heads' normal working week is an eight-performance week, divided among the six days, with no more than two performances a day. In addition to working the performance, some theater owners make arrangements with the house crew heads to be in attendance at the theater during part of the morning and afternoon. They maintain and repair elements of the theater structure.

The above is the normal weekly routine when a production is in residence. During the setting up, taking down, etc., *all* of them are in attendance at all times, even though only one department may be working. The house crew heads receive overtime during these periods, if work goes beyond regular working hours.

CASUALS.   Casuals work by the day and by the hour, or by the performance. For the setup, take-down, and such periods, there is a regular workday of a specified number of hours. If work extends beyond the regular workday, overtime is paid. If overtime exceeds a certain number of hours, or goes beyond a certain time of day, it becomes "extra overtime."

Casuals who work a performance are paid by the performance. A regular scale is set for eight performances a week. Extra performances have another scale. The performance is limited to three and one-half hours at the regular scale. These three and one-half hours include preperformance preparations, and after-performance stacking, storing, cleaning up, etc. Overtime is charged for performances that require more than three and one-half hours of work.

The term "minimum call" should be understood. It implies two things: (1) the minimum number of hands that must be used for a specified job, and (2) the minimum number of hours for which they receive payment.

EXAMPLE:

A special rehearsal is to be held. Only a portion of the scenery and properties is to be used, and only work lights are needed. The full complement of hands is not needed. A minimum call is established.

Minimum calls vary from job to job, from production to production, and from city to city.

BOX OFFICE

Box office treasurers are union men who have their own rules for working hours, number of men to be employed, use of the box office, etc. Moreover, they are bonded by insurance companies who also impose restrictions. In general, unauthorized persons—and that includes all actors and stage managers—are not permitted into the box office. Sometimes treasurers permit actors and stage managers to enter the box office in emergencies, such as to receive an emergency phone call. This courtesy should not be abused, and permission to make outgoing calls from the box office should not be requested. There should be no loitering around the box office.

MUSICIANS

Many Broadway legitimate shows do not use musicians in any capacity. The instances in which they are used, either as actual performers or as stand-bys, are treated as individual problems. Any rule given here would have so many exceptions, it would be confusing. The stage manager will have little or nothing to do with any problem concerning hiring of musicians. The business or company manager will handle this.

FRONT-OF-THE-HOUSE

Theater employees, such as ushers, porters, cleaning women, ticket-takers, doormen, and elevator operators are under the supervision of the house manager. Any contact the stage manager has with these employees should be made through the house manager.

E. Off-Broadway Stage Managing

A short explanation of the differences between Broadway
stage managing and stage managing for amateur, school,
university, little-theater, and stock company organizations

No one without proper training can expect to get a job as a
Broadway stage manager. However, lack of training should not
deter an aspirant for a stage manager's job with an off-Broadway
group. In fact, one of the aims of these groups is to give training. Another is to provide a hobby or extracurricular activity.
(The word "hobby" is used in the dictionary sense—"a subject or
pursuit in which a person takes persistent interest"—not with
any inference of frivolity or inconsequence. However, it does
imply that it is a nonwage-earning activity in these off-Broadway
groups.) Whatever the purpose of the off-Broadway group, anyone engaged in its work will want to do his job as well as he
can. To do a good job he will need sound training. If the reader
expects to find an esoteric formula or a handy short cut to replace
basic training, it is not known where he may look. He certainly
will not find it in this handbook. Training or knowledge must
come from experienced teachers or production personnel, from
proper textbooks on the elements of production, or from experimentation and experience. The stage manager must have a
thorough basic training, or be prepared to get it, because he can
accomplish his duties only to the limits of his training.

This handbook has given all the stage manager's duties for a
Broadway production. No attempt will be made here to give in
detail the duties of a stage manager for any or all types of off-

Broadway organizations. They are as varied and extensive as the organizations themselves. Fundamental differences between stage managing on Broadway and stage managing in schools, colleges, little theaters, and stock companies will be shown. It will be explained why these differences exist.

The stage manager for all organizations remains basically a liaison staff member. He differs from group to group in the balance of importance placed on his individual duties and on the amount of liaison work expected from him. This difference in emphasis comes about for several reasons. First, most off-Broadway groups produce established plays for a few performances and with a one-time aim. Second, they are the theater's main area for training, learning, and experimentation. Also, for many people, they serve as a hobby or extracurricular activity. Third, there is considerable difference between the Broadway and off-Broadway organization in the amount of time available for a production and the amount of labor the organization can afford.

I. Broadway stage managers of new and long-running plays face several problems that can be eliminated for off-Broadway stage managers because off-Broadway groups usually produce established and tested plays, and they have a one-time attitude. By "one-time" is not meant one performance. There may be just one or there may be a dozen performances. What is meant is that there is no emphasis on runs of many months or seasons. There is no planning or recording for the future of the production. The emotional drive for the production can be brought to a peak and then forgotten. There need be no effort to hold a high performance atmosphere over a long period. This relieves the production personnel of much of the work for the future that is demanded of a Broadway production staff, including the stage manager.

In most productions dialogue is established. The changes that may be made are usually very minor. Stage business, depending on the director, may be changed considerably or relatively little. This will be the only element of the prompt script that will concern the stage manager to any extent. Mood, emotion, characterization, tempo, and such things usually are not recorded, because a record of them is not needed. The various plots need not be constructed for long periods of reference, just for present needs. Thus, of the manuscript elements a stage manager tends, stage business and prompting receive the emphasis.

The off-Broadway stage manager rarely is concerned with understudies; or the rehearsal, costuming, or other problems they present.

Neither is "keeping the company fresh" a problem. Company rehearsals after the opening, replacements, or elaborate note-giving are infrequent. The necessity for repairs to physical elements seldom arises.

Touring, either in the tryout-tour or long-road-tour sense, is nonexistent.

Groups that produce new plays will need to add to their stage manager's job many of the duties facing the Broadway stage manager, but not met by school or stock stage managers. However, even in these groups, recording for the future may not be emphasized, and the emotional design is still the one-time type.

II. Many off-Broadway groups are established to train students, for experimentation or for hobby purposes. Consequently it sometimes happens that there may not be a member of the organization, other than the teacher or director, who is equipped with sufficient basic knowledge or time to be a well-rounded stage manager. This should not be considered a deficiency in these organizations. It is not. But it explains why many of these groups divide the duties of the stage manager among several persons. Unlike a Broadway director, the teacher or director of an off-Broadway group will sometimes take on many of the stage manager's activities. He may extend his job as "inspiriter" into that of a liaison staff member. He then retains much of this liaison duty for himself, and divides the purely functional duties of the stage manager among several persons. Consequently the staff of a production by an off-Broadway group may contain such members as the prompter, assistant to the director, stage manager in charge of lighting (or properties or scenery), and so on. These are necessary divisions of duties in many cases because no one person may have the ability or time to do a complete liaison-staff-member (stage managing) job. Moreover these divisions of work give more students or organization members an active part in the production. Also, as students assume the duties of Broadway's union stage hands, some of these student stage hand's duties may be stretched to include some of the stage manager's.

III. The problem of labor is important to these organizations. For those that are nonunion and noncommercial, or are training or hobby groups, the use of many persons is feasible and desirable. Their time and labor cost the organization nothing. The nature of the production and the organization's aims will be the guide in determining the use of personnel.

In stock companies, either union, partially union, or nonunion, the problems of salaries and time are very important. Most of them work with an extremely limited budget. The duties of the stage managers of these companies more nearly parallel those of the Broadway stage manager than those of other off-Broadway groups. However, stock stage managers are among those who have less emphasis placed on their manuscript duties, and who also have the advantage of being with an organization which has a one-time attitude. This balance of importance gives the stage manager more time and energy to divert into other duties. And so, among his regular duties, he may include lighting, acting, finding and preparing properties, and other things. From stock company to stock company, from production to production, the difference will not be so much in what his duties are, but in what balance of importance is given them. He remains a liaison staff member, ready to balance the production scales as required.

INDEX